SPOTLIGHT

COEUR D'ALENE & THE IDAHO PANHANDLE

JAMES P. KELLY

Contents

COEUR D'ALENE & THE IDAHO PANHANDLE

THE PANHANDLE

Idaho's Panhandle is shimmed like a log wedge between Montana, Washington, and British Columbia. This stovepipe-shaped section of the Gem State is a mere 45 miles wide at its skinniest swath, but what the Panhandle lacks in landmass, it more than makes up for with a multitude of large glacial lakes and densely forested mountains.

The booming resort towns of Coeur d'Alene and Sandpoint bring in the lion's share of local tourism thanks to their prime real estate on Idaho's two largest lakes: Coeur d'Alene and Pend Oreille. But much of the region is remote and unpopulated, just a few miles on either side of the busy I-90 and U.S. 95 corridors.

Outdoor recreation abounds in north Idaho. White-water rafting near Bonners Ferry; hiking and mountain biking in the Selway-Bitterroot Wilderness; shredding morning powder at Silver Mountain; and cruising the sky-blue waterways in old wooden boats keep locals busy year-round, and they don't mind sharing their wondrous playground with others.

People in the Panhandle are unabashedly independent, and friendly to boot. The state capital in Boise seems like a world away, and many folks here don't think that secession is such a bad idea. Why do you think they call it "north Idaho" instead of northern Idaho? Independent sovereignty probably won't happen anytime soon, but the Panhandle is definitely far removed from other parts of the state.

Historic sights are intertwined along the trodden pathways. The old mission in Cataldo, just east of Coeur d'Alene in Silver Valley, offers glimpses into Idaho's early Catholic

© IDAHO DIVISION OF TOURISM

HIGHLIGHTS

◖ **Tubbs Hill:** This gorgeous 120-acre nature preserve on Coeur d'Alene Lake is a Frisbee fling away from downtown Coeur d'Alene (page 11).

◖ **Old Mission State Park:** It may be small, but this state park in Cataldo boasts a beautiful Greek Revival-style mission, the oldest existing building in Idaho (page 26).

◖ **Wallace:** Old mining towns don't get any funkier than Wallace, which is so historic that the entire town is on the National Register of Historic Places (page 31).

◖ **Silverwood Theme Park:** People from across the Northwest flock here for wild amusement park rides, like the 55-mph wooden roller coaster aptly named Timber Terror (page 35).

◖ **Schweitzer Mountain Resort:** This all-season resort near Sandpoint has the most stunning views in the Panhandle. The skiing and snowboarding is remarkable too (page 47).

◖ **Priest Lake State Park:** Idaho's northernmost state park has three units, two of which are on Priest Lake's pristine east shore (page 51).

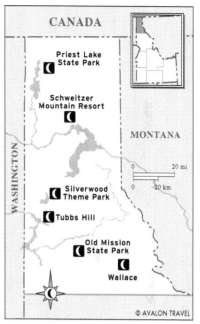

LOOK FOR ◖ TO FIND RECOMMENDED SIGHTS, ACTIVITIES, DINING, AND LODGING.

culture, which sought to bring Coeur d'Alene Indians into its fold in the mid-1900s. Nearby, travelers will marvel at the Victorian architecture and sheer funkiness of Wallace, a lovingly restored mining town with a taste for debauchery. A profusion of antiques shops, old saloons, and strange museums make this place one of the most interesting stops in the Panhandle, or in Idaho, for that matter.

To the far north, Priest Lake shimmers like a bright diamond below sharp mountain peaks. Ancient cedar and hemlock forests line the shore, and huckleberry bushes are just about everywhere you look, including on local menus in late summer.

PLANNING YOUR TIME

The Panhandle is the state's smallest region in terms of square miles, but it offers some of the best resorts and recreational opportunities in Idaho, most of which are easily accessible from I-90 and U.S. 95. Allow yourself at least a week to explore the area. Coeur d'Alene and Sandpoint are good base camps.

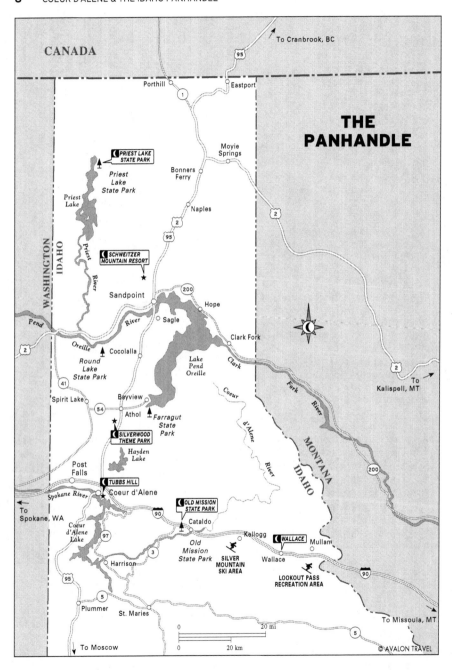

Coeur d'Alene and Vicinity

Shortly after the Mullan Road opened the Panhandle to miners and settlers, U.S. Army general William Tecumseh Sherman came through scouting locations for a new fort. The Army wanted a north Idaho base to protect the burgeoning white populace from Native American attack and to make sure the Brits didn't push their way south of the 49th parallel. In 1878, construction of Fort Coeur d'Alene began.

The fort, and the town that grew around it, were named for the local Native Americans. Although they called themselves *Schitsu'umsh,* meaning "The Ones That Were Found Here," the French trappers called them the *coeur d'alène*—"heart like an awl." Authorities agree the name arose from the Native Americans' shrewd trading abilities but argue whether the trappers coined the phrase first or adopted it after hearing the Native Americans use it to describe the French. In any case, the name stuck. After

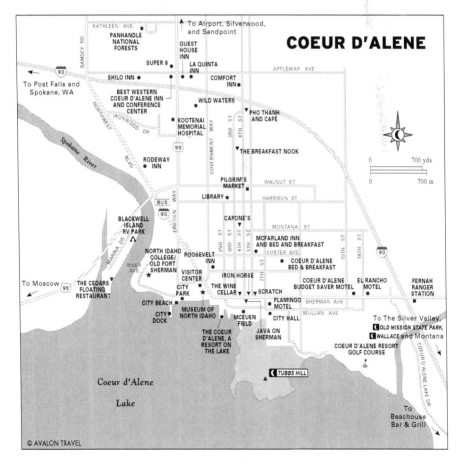

Sherman died, the fort's name was changed to honor him, but the town that grew around the fort kept the moniker Coeur d'Alene. In the 1880s the town became the lake's biggest steamship port; ships carried passengers and supplies to and from the booming Coeur d'Alene Mining District and communities around the lake.

Today, Coeur d'Alene (population 44,000) ranks as the top resort town in the inland Northwest. In summer, the long lakefront boardwalk bustles with bikini-clad sun worshippers, Frisbee-fetching dogs, ice cream–licking youngsters, and busloads of camera-toting tourists. Out on the lake, Jet Skis buzz and flit like hopped-up waterborne mosquitoes while water-skiers race the wakes of the cruise boats, and parasailers brighten the skies overhead. No question—this city is alive and exciting in summer.

In winter the crowds disappear, and a quiet, intense beauty descends with the first snowfall. Skiers make the morning commute out to one of the region's three downhill resorts, while bald eagles—intent on fattening up on the lake's abundant kokanee salmon—make their annual pilgrimage to Wolf Lodge Bay. It's a great season to relax at one of the town's numerous bed-and-breakfasts—to sit by a crackling fire, pick up a good book, and drift off to dreams of spring.

SIGHTS
North Idaho College and Old Fort Sherman

The campus of this two-year junior college (1000 W. Garden Ave., 208/769-3300, www. nic.edu) occupies the grounds of old Fort Sherman, one of the major military installations in the Northwest from 1878 to 1901. It was from here that troops were dispatched up the Silver Valley to quell the mining wars of 1892. Today only a few structures from the fort remain, scattered among modern school buildings. The campus is a nice place to just poke around on, thanks to its prime lakefront real estate, expansive lawns, and big evergreens.

Museum of North Idaho

Kootenai County's history is featured at the Museum of North Idaho (115 Northwest Blvd., Coeur d'Alene, 208/664-3448, www. museumni.org, 11 A.M.–5 P.M. Tues.–Sat. Apr.–Oct.), in front of City Park. Exhibit topics include the Mullan Road, Fort Sherman, early transportation—including railroads and steamboats—and local industry, especially logging and mining.

An annex, the **Fort Sherman Museum,** on the North Idaho College campus (W. Garden Ave. and N. College Dr., Coeur d'Alene, 1–4:45 P.M. Tues.–Sat. May–Sept.), has exhibits including a 1924 smoke-chaser's cabin, a model of old Fort Sherman, and a lifeboat from the *Miss Spokane*—a passenger boat that plied Coeur d'Alene Lake in the 1920s. The museum provides a walking-tour brochure to the several Fort Sherman structures that have been preserved.

A single admission of $3 adults, $1 ages 6–16, $7 family is valid for both museums.

Sightseeing Tours
SIGHTSEEING CRUISES

Lake Coeur d'Alene Cruises (208/765-4000, www.cdalakecruises.com) offers 90-minute tours of the lake (daily late Apr.–late Oct., $19.75 adults, $17.75 seniors, $11.75 ages 6–12). Also available are Sunday brunch cruises, Pirates of the Coeur d'Alene cruises, and a Fourth of July fireworks cruise. All public cruises leave from City Dock at Independence Point, next to the Coeur d'Alene Resort.

Another motorized way to tour the lake is offered by **Bobby D's Custom Tours** (208/667-0807 or 208/699-7206, www.lake-coeurdalenecruise.com), a year-round charter service offering private trips aboard its 26-foot Alumaweld cabin cruiser, *The Joanna*. Especially awesome are the bald eagle viewing cruises (Nov.–Feb.), where you'll see dozens of these majestic birds hanging out in old snags along the shoreline. For $100 per hour with a two-hour minimum, you can charter the boat helmed by an experienced captain.

ON GUARD FOR HUMAN RIGHTS

Idaho – especially the state's Panhandle region – has long had a reputation as a haven for racists, but events in recent years show that perceptions and reality may both be turning.

From 1973, Richard Butler ruled the white-supremacist Aryan Nations organization from a compound in Hayden, Idaho, a few miles north of Coeur d'Alene. The ultraright-wing racist and his followers were an unending source of embarrassment to the vast majority of north Idahoans. Groups including the Kootenai County Task Force on Human Relations and the Human Rights Education Institute spoke out strongly against the Aryan Nations' presence in their backyard.

Finally, in 2000, Butler was forced into bankruptcy by a $6.3 million civil judgment resulting from a suit filed by the Southern Poverty Law Center on behalf of an Idaho woman and her son who said Butler's group shot at them in 1998. Philanthropist Greg Carr, an Idaho native, purchased Butler's compound and donated it to the North Idaho College Foundation, which now operates the Hayden Lake site as a **peace park.** Groups wishing to visit can make an appointment by calling 208/769-5978. Meanwhile, the Human Rights Education Institute, again aided by a donation from Carr, opened a human rights interpretive center (414 Mullan Ave., Coeur d'Alene, 208/292-2359, www.hrei.org) in a historic building in downtown Coeur d'Alene's City Park. The center features permanent and traveling human rights' exhibits, educational programs, and community outreach.

A small fuel charge applies. All cruises leave from City Dock.

FLIGHTSEEING

Brooks Sea Plane (208/664-2842 or 208/659-1511, www.brooks-seaplane.com) takes passengers aloft on 20-minute sightseeing flights around the lake ($60 adults, $30 under age 12). You'll fly aboard either a float-equipped Cessna 206 or a gorgeous seven-passenger De Havilland Beaver, the bush pilot's workhorse. The planes leave from City Dock on Independence Point, next to the Coeur d'Alene Resort. Longer flights are also available. **Big Country Helicopters** (208/765-0620, www.bigcountryhelicopters.com) offers chopper hops (from $130 pp) of a half-hour or longer around the area.

RECREATION
◖ Tubbs Hill

One of the city's highlights, this beautiful 120-acre wooded preserve (free) juts out into the lake right next to the Coeur d'Alene Resort. Trails loop around the peninsula through groves of Douglas fir and century-old ponderosa pine. Some paths climb up the hill for panoramic views; others drop down to hidden coves and beaches. It's all a city park, open to foot traffic only and within easy walking distance of anywhere downtown. The best time to enjoy Tubbs Hill is during an after-dinner stroll, when you can walk off your meal and enjoy a gorgeous sunset at the same time. For more information, contact the Coeur d'Alene Parks Department (710 E. Mullan Ave., Coeur d'Alene, 208/769-2252).

Biking and Skating

The **North Idaho Centennial Trail,** a 23-mile hiking, biking, and skating trail, stretches west from Higgins Point on Coeur d'Alene Lake's northeast shore through the cities of Coeur d'Alene and Post Falls to the Washington state line. Ambitious folks can continue west on the abutting Spokane River Centennial Trail; it's another 22 miles to Spokane. For most of its length, the trail is either completely separated from traffic or off on a big, wide shoulder. Animals on leashes are allowed, and interpretive signs mark many points of interest along the way. You can pick up the trail at City Park, downtown, or on Coeur d'Alene Lake Drive.

Swimming and Sunbathing

When those sunny summer days roll around, **City Beach** is the place to be. The water warms up enough for swimming and splashing, and the beach, boardwalk, and adjacent **City Park** fill with skaters, Frisbee-throwers, joggers, swimmers, gawkers, and gawkees—the people-watching can't be beat.

If the tame lakeshore bores you, head to **Wild Waters** (2119 N. Government Way, Coeur d'Alene, 208/667-6491, www.wildwaterswaterpark.com, $25 over 48 inches, $20 under 48 inches, $13 seniors and disabled, free under age 3) near I-90. This recently renovated waterslide theme park also has a grassy area for sunning, hot pools for soaking, a video arcade, and a snack bar. The park is open the last two weekends in May (including Memorial Day Monday), then daily the first weekend in June–early September. Hours are 11 A.M.–6 P.M., 11 A.M.–7 P.M. in midsummer. Parents can get a viewing-only pass for $13, which allows them to keep an eye on Junior without getting wet themselves.

Parasailing

On sunny summer afternoons, the blue skies over Lake Coeur d'Alene are complemented by the brightly colored chutes of **Coeur d'Alene Parasail** (208/765-2999, www.cdaparasail.net, 10 A.M.–7 P.M. Sun.–Fri., solo $60, tandem $90). You'll be towed 400 or more feet in the air behind a speedboat for an 8–10-minute ride over the lake. And thanks to the specially designed boat and hydraulic winch system, you won't even get wet.

Boat Rentals

Boardwalk Marina at the Coeur d'Alene Resort (208/765-4000) rents 20-foot speedboats for $125 per hour with a two-hour minimum. Tax and fuel are additional, and you'll have to leave a credit card for a deposit.

On the other side of the dock, **Island Rentals** (208/666-1626) rents out Jet Skis

during the summer months. Expect to pay around $85 per hour (fuel and lifejacket included) for one of these little zippers.

You'll also find more humble people-powered canoes, paddleboats, and such available for rent at City Dock in summer.

Fishing

Coeur d'Alene Lake has hungry populations of kokanee, chinook salmon, and northern pike. **Fins & Feathers** (1816 Sherman Ave., Coeur d'Alene, 208/667-9304), a tackle shop and guide service, can help you find the biggest ones and provide the boat and all equipment as well. The going rate for a party of two is $325 for a half-day trip, $495 for a full day.

While the big lake is the obvious centerpiece of the area, don't forget 300-acre **Fernan Lake,** east of I-90 at the Sherman exit, where you can fish for wild cutthroat trout and stocked rainbows as well as warm-water species like largemouth bass, crappie, perch, and catfish. In winter you can probe beneath the frozen crust, primarily for perch. Boat ramps and docks are found at either end of the lake.

Golf

The star attraction for Coeur d'Alene linksters is **Coeur d'Alene Resort Golf Course** (900 Floating Green Dr., Coeur d'Alene, 208/667-4653, www.cdaresort.com, nonguests from $175). The beautiful lakeside course boasts a great gimmick: The 14th hole features a moveable floating green. A cute little putt-putt boat ferries you out to it, assuming your ball actually made it to the green and isn't on its way to Davey Jones's locker. Aim carefully.

All the golf magazines rave about the 6,804-yard, par-71 course, designed by Scott Miller and extensively renovated in 2003 with 500 new yards to play. Guests of the resort get a major price break and a free water-taxi ride from the hotel to the course. Rates include a cart and caddie. Clubs and golf shoes can be rented. No plebes, please: "Proper attire is required at all times," reads the rule, "Men—slacks or suitable length shorts and shirts with sleeves and collars.

Women—dresses, skirts and blouses, slacks, culottes, or proper length shorts."

Humbler courses in town include **Coeur d'Alene Golf Club** (2201 S. Fairway Dr., Coeur d'Alene, 208/765-0218, about $28), a 6,274-yard, par-72 course, and **Ponderosa Springs Golf Course** (1291 N. Galena Dr., Coeur d'Alene, 208/664-1101, about $12), a nine-hole course.

White-Water Rafting

You won't find any white-water rivers in the Coeur d'Alene area, but you will find **ROW Adventures** (202 Sherman Ave., Coeur d'Alene, 208/765-0841 or 800/451-6034, www. rowadventures.com), one of Idaho's biggest and best rafting companies. The company runs all the Idaho standards—the Snake River through Hells Canyon, the Salmon, the Middle Fork Salmon, the Lochsa, and the Selway Rivers—plus lesser-known white water like the Moyie, Clark Fork, St. Joe, and Owyhee Rivers. ROW is an acronym for both River Odysseys West and Remote Odysseys Worldwide; in addition to domestic rivers, the company runs raft trips in Ecuador, barge trips on French canals, yacht trips along the Turkish coast, trekking trips in Nepal, and more.

Backcountry Hiking and Mountain Biking

The U.S. Forest Service's **Coeur d'Alene River Ranger District** Fernan Ranger Station (2502 E. Sherman Ave., Coeur d'Alene, 208/769-3000) is on the east side of I-90. Stop by for information on nearby backcountry hiking and biking opportunities. The Forest Service publishes descriptive flyers on several hiking trails, primarily found deep in the Coeur d'Alene Mountains between Hayden Lake, Lake Pend Oreille, and the upper North Fork of the Coeur d'Alene River. A couple of trails to the east begin closer to town, around the Wolf Lodge District. In addition, logging roads lace the nearby mountains; just continue east from the Fernan Ranger Station on Fernan Lake Road, which skirts the north shore of the lake and then climbs up toward Huckleberry

Mountain. Past that point, dirt roads suitable for hiking or mountain biking spin off in every direction. Inquire at the ranger station to find out which, if any, of these roads are being actively logged.

CANFIELD MOUNTAIN TRAIL SYSTEM

The Canfield Mountain Trail System is part of the web of logging roads mentioned above. Its 32 miles of single- and double-track trails are open to hikers, equestrians, motorcycles, and mountain bikes; fat-tire bicyclists currently make best use of the area. Several access points are available along Forest Road 1562, which links Nettleton Gulch Road with Fernan Lake Road in a meandering, roundabout fashion. Nettleton Gulch Road intersects 15th Street 1.1 miles north of I-90 Exit 14, becoming Forest Road 1562 farther east. On the east side, Forest Road 1562 intersects Fernan Lake Road 5.5 miles east of I-90 Exit 15. Pick up a map to the trail system at the Fernan Ranger Station.

Skiing

Although Coeur d'Alene has no downhill ski areas to call its own, several are close enough for a day trip. North up U.S. 95 about 50 miles is **Schweitzer Mountain,** high in the Selkirks overlooking Sandpoint and Lake Pend Oreille. To the east on I-90 are **Silver Mountain**—40 miles from town at Kellogg and home of the world's longest gondola—and **Lookout Pass,** 20 miles beyond that at the Montana border. Popular cross-country areas in the vicinity include **Fourth of July Pass Park N' Ski Area,** 18 miles east of Coeur d'Alene at Fourth of July Pass, and Farragut and Round Lake State Parks to the north.

Outfitters

Vertical Earth (2175 N. Main St., Coeur d'Alene, 208/667-5503, www.verticalearth. com, daily) rents out mountain bikes, snowboards, snowshoes, and cross-country skis, including telemark demo gear. And you're not too far from mega-outfitter **REI** (1125 N. Monroe St., Spokane, WA, 509/328-9900, www.rei. com), just over the border in Washington.

ENTERTAINMENT AND EVENTS

Nightlife

The **Iron Horse** (407 E. Sherman Ave., Coeur d'Alene, 208/667-7314) in downtown Coeur d'Alene is the place to go for drinks and dancing. This venerable nightspot features live music (usually rock and country) on weekends. The Iron Horse also has a full-service restaurant serving breakfast, lunch, and dinner daily.

Performing Arts

North Idaho College sponsors the bulk of the area's concerts and dramatic performances, like the Coeur d'Alene Summer Theatre. For current listings, call the college's **Boswell Hall Schuler Performing Arts Center** (208/769-7780). The **Citizens' Council for the Arts** (208/667-9346, www.artonthegreen.org) has lots of information on the region's fine and performing arts scene.

Events

Highlights of the town's events calendar include **Fred Murphy Days,** the last weekend in May, honoring a locally legendary steamboat captain with good food and drink, contests of strength and skill, street dances, a parade, and a good deal of giddiness; **Fourth of July,** which brings an Independence Day parade to beat the band; **Art on the Green** (www.artonthegreen.org) at North Idaho College in early August; and the **Coeur d'Alene Wooden Boat Festival** (www.coeurdalene.org/woodenboatshow.htm), which beautifies the lake the third weekend in August. From the weekend following Thanksgiving until after New Year's Day, the Coeur d'Alene Resort area and lakeside boardwalks glow with more than 1 million **holiday lights.** For more information about area events, call Coeur d'Alene Chamber of Commerce (208/664-3194, www.cdachamber.com).

SHOPPING

For an excellent selection of regional art, check out **Art Spirit Gallery** (415 Sherman Ave., Coeur d'Alene, 208/765-6006, www. theartspiritgallery.com, 11 A.M.–6 P.M. daily summer) downtown, which offers great stuff from about 30 established and emerging artists from the Idaho Panhandle, Washington, and Montana. Featured artists include George Carlson, nationally known for his monumental sculptures, and Russell Chatham.

Fans of antiques and collectibles will have a field day here. The phone book is chock-full of dealers and antiques malls. Check out the lovably funky **Wiggett's Antiques Marketplace** (115 S. 4th Ave., Coeur d'Alene, 208/664-1524) next to Coeur d'Alene Resort.

Also downtown, you'll find a handful of cool stores in Coeur d'Alene Resort's **Plaza Shops** (210 E. Sherman Ave., Coeur d'Alene), including **Papillon Paper Emporium** (208/664-0736) and **Bruttles** (208/664-6586), which sells truffles and other chocolate treats.

The biggest shopping mall in town is **Silver Lake Mall** (200 W. Hanley Ave., Coeur d'Alene, 208/762-2112, 10 A.M.–9 P.M. Mon.–Sat., 11 A.M.–6 P.M. Sun.), north of I-90 on either U.S. 95 or Government Way, with 50 stores that include Sears, JC Penney, and Macy's.

ACCOMMODATIONS

Sherman Avenue runs between Coeur d'Alene Resort and I-90 on the east side of town. A number of mostly inexpensive–moderate older independent motels are along this strip. The area has the advantage of being surrounded by quiet old residential areas and being near funky, character-filled shops and restaurants. On the west end, the lodgings are within easy walking distance of downtown; on the east end, you'll be near I-90.

The other motel district is along Appleway Avenue, which parallels I-90 to the north. This area has the advantages of being close to I-90 and being surrounded by modern shopping malls and fast-food emporiums, which are also the disadvantages. Most of the major chain motels are here.

$50-100

The **Budget Saver Motel Coeur d'Alene** (1519 Sherman Ave., Coeur d'Alene, 208/667-9505,

$50–120) doesn't look like much from the outside, but it's well worth the low prices—among the cheapest in town. The rooms are decent, and some have two bedrooms—a nice touch for added privacy. In the same area, you'll find **El Rancho Motel** (1915 Sherman Ave., Coeur d'Alene, 208/664-8794, $39–75), which has 14 standard rooms.

If you want to be a few blocks from the lake, try the **⟨ Flamingo Motel** (718 Sherman Ave., Coeur d'Alene, 208/664-2159 or 800/955-2159, www.flamingomotelidaho.com, from $90 d), a gussied-up motor inn with a pool and some kitchenettes.

Over on Appleway Avenue, you'll find **Super 8** (505 W. Appleway Ave., Coeur d'Alene, 208/765-8880 or 800/800-8000, from $66 d); **La Quinta Inn** (280 W. Appleway Ave., Coeur d'Alene, 208/765-5500, from $74 d); and **GuestHouse Inn** (330 W. Appleway Ave., Coeur d'Alene, 208/765-3011, from $89 d).

A few miles north of town on U.S. 95 is **Silver Lake Motel** (6160 Sunshine St., Coeur d'Alene, 208/772-8595 or 800/732-8094, www.silverlakemotel.com, from $56), with amenities like an outdoor pool, a lounge, and free continental breakfast.

$100–150

Among the plushest places in town are the **Shilo Inn** (702 W. Appleway Ave., Coeur d'Alene, 208/664-2300 or 800/222-2244, from $139 d), which offers all minisuites with kitchenettes, and the **Best Western Coeur d'Alene Inn and Conference Center** (506 W. Appleway Ave., Coeur d'Alene, 208/765-3200 or 800/251-7829, from $129 d), a full-service hotel with an indoor pool and spa. Both hotels sometimes have guest rooms for under $100.

Coeur d'Alene is the bed-and-breakfast capital of Idaho; about a dozen are sprinkled throughout town, with a half-dozen more in the outlying areas. Unless specified, the B&Bs below serve a full breakfast, don't permit children under 12 or pets, and don't allow smoking indoors. Note that B&B prices vary widely with the particular guest room rented,

and some places have guest rooms that exceed this price category. For more listings of area B&Bs, visit the North Idaho Bed and Breakfast Association's website (www.nibba.com).

East of town, off the lake's north shore, **⟨ Katie's Wild Rose Inn** (7974 E. Coeur d'Alene Lake Dr., Coeur d'Alene, 208/765-9474 or 800/371-4345, www.katieswildroseinn.com, $89–200) sits high on a promontory overlooking Bennett Bay. Wild roses grace the grounds, and a rose motif runs throughout the interior. The inn sits alongside the Centennial Trail bike path. Of the four guest rooms, two have private baths and two share a bath. One has an in-room jetted tub.

⟨ The Roosevelt Inn Bed & Breakfast (105 E. Wallace Ave., Coeur d'Alene, 208/765-5200 or 800/290-3358, www.therooseveltinn.com, $119–279) occupies the redbrick 1906 Roosevelt School, which was converted in 1994. All guest rooms have private baths and are furnished with antiques; some guest rooms have a lake view. Common areas include a small exercise center and two parlors—one with a TV and Internet access, the other a quiet room for reading or writing. Rates include a gourmet full breakfast.

The McFarland Inn Bed & Breakfast (601 E. Foster Ave., Coeur d'Alene, 208/667-1232 or 800/335-1232, www.mcfarlandinn.com, $135–165) offers five guest rooms in a graceful turn-of-the-20th-century home furnished with both elegant antiques and modern amenities. A gourmet breakfast and afternoon tea are served daily, and fresh coffee and goodies are always available. Each guest room has a private bath with a claw-foot tub and a shower. Children over 14 are welcome.

Just west of town in a tranquil country setting is **American Country Bed & Breakfast** (705 Zircon Lane, Coeur d'Alene, 877/664-9650, www.americancountrybedandbreakfast.com, $125–215). This Americana-inspired inn offers a big deck, a big breakfast, and big smiles from its hosts Brian and Shar Scott. The B&B has three guest rooms and a cottage made to look like a tree house. Children and pets are not allowed, and smoking is permitted outside.

Over $250

By many people's standards, **The Coeur d'Alene, a Resort on the Lake** (115 S. 2nd St., Coeur d'Alene, 208/765-4000 or 800/688-5253, www.cdaresort.com), owned by publishing magnate Duane Hagadone, is *the* hotel in Idaho. It seems to be a pet of travel writers; the resort gets a lot of press and has been included more than once on *Condé Nast Traveler* magazine's "Gold List" of the world's best hotels. It definitely ranks high in terms of location, rising into the sky over the shores of exquisitely beautiful Coeur d'Alene Lake, and it offers a mind-boggling array of extravagant amenities. With all that in mind, is there any room for disagreement with the glowing reviews? Does anyone dare not like this place? Yes, and yes. One wonders what architect R. G. Nelson was thinking, putting a skyscraper on a beautiful lakeshore. Unlike, say, Yosemite's Ahwahnee Hotel, this big tan monster doesn't complement the environment, it competes with it, resembling nothing so much as a giant tower of Legos. In addition, although codeveloper Jerry Jaeger was once quoted as saying, "This will be a place to come and play; nobody's going to wear a tie," the self-conscious "informality" here is cloaked in Gucci and Chanel, and you'll feel out of place in jeans. Standard guest rooms usually run $250 or more in summer; pay much less and you risk getting a depressing "economy" room that'll make you wish you stayed at Motel 6 for half the price. The high-end guest rooms can fetch as much as $499 in summer. Lower prices are offered in the off-season. Spa, ski, golf, and other packages are available.

Vacation Rental Companies

Coeur d'Alene Vacation (509/954-6111, www.cdavacation.com) lists year-round vacation home rentals, some on the lake. **Resort Property Management** (2120 N. 3rd St., Coeur d'Alene, 208/667-6035, www.resort-propertiesidaho.com) has listings for more than 75 summer cabins in the $100–500 per night range.

CAMPING AND RVING

Blackwell Island RV Park (800 S. Marina Dr., Coeur d'Alene, 208/665-1300 or 888/571-2900, $35–46 with full hookups) is a large park with boat docks and grassy pull-throughs just across the Spokane River from town: Take U.S. 95 south one mile from I-90 and turn left on Marina Drive.

River Walk RV Park (1214 Mill Ave., at Northwest Blvd., Coeur d'Alene, 208/765-5943 or 888/567-8700, $22–36) offers 42 sites with full hookups. The park has showers, restrooms, and a laundry room.

FOOD
Upscale Fare

Beverly's (115 S. 2nd St., Coeur d'Alene, 208/765-4000, www.cdaresort.com, lunch and dinner daily, entrées $24–55) is the Coeur d'Alene Resort's premier dining room, on the hotel's seventh floor overlooking the lake. On the menu you'll find entrées that make optimum use of fresh Northwestern ingredients in high-cuisine fashion. The restaurant maintains a huge wine cellar; chances are they'll have exactly what you're looking for.

The Cedars Floating Restaurant (208/664-2922, www.cedarsfloatingrestaurant.com, dinner from 4 P.M. daily, $22–39) is also affiliated with Coeur d'Alene Resort. This is the place to go for fresh fish and romantic atmosphere. To get here, head south on U.S. 95 toward Moscow. On the edge of town, turn left onto Marina Drive immediately after crossing the Spokane River. This takes you out onto Blackwell Island, an area of working boat shops and boat storage yards. The restaurant is all the way out at the tip of the island, moored where the Spokane River flows out of Coeur d'Alene Lake. Fish entrées vary, depending on availability, but might include wild salmon, swordfish, halibut, or ahi; some are grilled, others cooked on a cedar plank. Poultry, pasta, steaks, and rack of lamb are also available.

For fine Italian dining, make a reservation at **Angelo's Ristorante** (846 N. 4th St., Coeur d'Alene, 208/765-2850, www.angelosristorante.net, lunch 11 A.M.–4 P.M.

Mon.–Fri., dinner 5–10 P.M. daily, $14–25). Here you'll find a classic Mediterranean dining room and upscale preparations of antipasto, pasta, risotto, scampi, steaks, and rack of lamb. Expect to see a big wine list of Italian and Washington labels.

€ Scratch (501 E. Sherman Ave., Coeur d'Alene, 208/930-4762, lunch 11 A.M.–3 P.M. Mon.–Fri., dinner 3–10 P.M. Mon.–Thurs., 3–11 P.M. Fri.–Sat., dinner entrées $16–38) is a global fusion restaurant and lounge downtown that uses local foodstuffs in a creative manner. The menu changes with the season and availability of products. The dinner menu leans toward Asia and the Mediterranean for inspiration.

Casual Dining

Capone's Pub & Grill (751 N. 4th St., Coeur d'Alene, 208/667-4843, www.caponespub.com, lunch and dinner daily) entices beer drinkers with some two dozen Northwestern microbrews on tap. The decor is vintage sports, with old baseball mitts, skis, golf clubs, and ice skates hanging from the ceiling and historical sports photos lining the walls, including one of…Jerry Garcia? Seems there's a Deadhead subplot in the bullpen. Whatever game you're looking for, you'll probably find it on one of the five TVs connected to two satellite dishes. The friendly and comfortable place also serves an extensive menu of first-class pub grub, including burgers, subs, and creative, made-from-scratch gourmet pizzas (try the Thai chicken variation). Live entertainment several nights a week draws a fun crowd. Capone's is well worth the short hop up from downtown.

The **Beachouse Bar & Grill** (3204 Coeur d'Alene Lake Dr., Coeur d'Alene, 208/664-6464, dinner daily, $12–22), at the north shore's Silver Bay Marina, serves steaks, seafood, barbecued ribs, and pasta. You're paying a lot for atmosphere—this is one of only two places in town right on the water—and for the restaurant's association with the Hagadone Corporation. The resort's guests are chauffeured here by boat, which no doubt adds to

the overhead. Still, this is a good place for a lakeside dinner, preferably out on the deck.

€ Bistro on Spruce (1710 N. 4th St., Coeur d'Alene, 208/664-1774, www.bistroonspruce.com, lunch 11 A.M.–2:30 P.M. Mon.–Fri., dinner 5–9 P.M. Mon.–Thurs., 5–10 P.M. Fri.–Sat., entrées $13–23) is a casual new restaurant with a decidedly Mediterranean menu. Expect to find Guinness onion soup, mushroom risotto, paella (saffron rice with sausage and seafood), and pan-roasted duck breast with Marsala reduction. Oh, yeah, there are lots of microbrews and wines by the glass.

Wine Bars

€ The Wine Cellar (313 Sherman Ave., Coeur d'Alene, 208/664-9463, 4:30–10 P.M. Mon.–Thurs., 4:30 P.M.–midnight Fri.–Sat.) is a venerable downtown wine bar that features live jazz nightly. The wine list has more than 250 worldwide labels, which play well with the Mediterranean menu. The sidewalk patio is a great place to people-watch while sipping syrah and noshing on tapas.

Just down the street, you'll find **Barrel Room No. 6** (503 E. Sherman Ave., Coeur d'Alene, 208/664-9632, 4 P.M.–late Wed.–Fri., 2 P.M.–late Sat.), which is Coeur d'Alene Cellars' wine bar. You can taste the winery's vintages in a stylish space with big sofas and wine-barrel furniture. This happening little place supplements its wine list with microbrews and a light menu of appetizers and desserts. Coeur d'Alene Cellars (3890 N. Schreiber Way, Coeur d'Alene, 208/664-2336, www.cdacellars.com, tasting room 11 A.M.–5 P.M. Tues.–Sat.) also has a tasting room at the winery, where it produces several remarkable varietal wines and blends made from Columbia Valley grapes.

Ethnic Cuisine

Sushi fans will surely like **Takara Japanese Restaurant & Sushi Bar** (309 Lakeside Ave., Coeur d'Alene, 208/765-8014, www.cda-sushi.com, lunch and dinner daily). This downtown restaurant puts out a large selection of maki rolls, nigiri, and sashimi. You also can get hot

a sampling of produce at the Kootenai County Farmers Market in Coeur d'Alene

© DANA HOPPER-KELLY

offerings like tempura, sukiyaki, and teriyaki. Don't worry, there's plenty of sake and Japanese rice lager to wash everything down.

If you're craving a bowl of pho (Vietnamese beef noodle soup), head to **Pho Thanh & Café** (2108 N. 4th St., Coeur d'Alene, 208/665-9903, lunch and dinner daily, around $10), a little Vietnamese restaurant near I-90. The servers can be rude at times, but the kitchen pumps out decent Southeast Asian standards such as pho, crispy spring rolls, steamed rice plates, and vermicelli noodle dishes.

For standard Mexican fare, check out **Toro Viejo** (117 N. 2nd St., Coeur d'Alene, 208/667-7676, lunch and dinner daily, around $10). This festive downtown eatery dishes up enchiladas, tacos, burritos, and fajitas. The restaurant also serves margaritas and Mexican beers.

Breakfast and Coffee

The Breakfast Nook (1719 N. 4th St., Coeur d'Alene, 208/667-1699, 6 A.M.–2 P.M. Mon.–Sat., 7 A.M.–2 P.M. Sun., under $10) is the place for big American-style breakfasts. The menu has steak and eggs, French toast, eggs Benny, pancakes, and omelets galore.

Downtown, 【 **Java on Sherman** (324 Sherman Ave., Coeur d'Alene, 208/667-0010, 6 A.M.–8 P.M. Sun.–Wed., 6 A.M.–9 P.M. Fri.–Sat.) is a clean, well-lighted place to enjoy great joe while reading Hemingway or writing the great American novel. Big front windows command the best people-watching corner in north Idaho, and many caffeine-laced concoctions are available; go for the trademark Bowl of Soul (espresso in steamed milk topped with chocolate and cinnamon). The pastries are baked on the premises. Bigger breakfasts are available too. Both the atmosphere and the help are young, hip, and friendly.

Groceries

Pilgrim's Market (1316 N. 4th St., Coeur d'Alene, 208/676-9730, www.pilgrimsmarket.com, 9 A.M.–8 P.M. daily) is a natural food store that specializes in organic local produce, meats, and bread. The market also has bulk foods, dietary supplements, and earthy beauty products.

Head to the bustling downtown **Kootenai County Farmers Market** (5th St. and Sherman Ave., Coeur d'Alene, 4–7 P.M. Wed. May–Sept.) for impeccably fresh local produce and meats, honey, salsa, eggs, and artisanal bread. You also can get hot food like wood-fired pizzas and lamb burgers, plus there's live music.

INFORMATION AND SERVICES

Coeur d'Alene Chamber of Commerce's **Visitors Bureau** (105 N. 1st St., Coeur d'Alene, 208/664-3194, www.coeurdalene. org) is conveniently located downtown across from City Park. It's well stocked with maps and brochures on lodging, restaurants, and recreation.

Recreation information for most of north Idaho is available from the Supervisor's Office of the **Idaho Panhandle National Forests** (3815 Schreiber Way, Coeur d'Alene, 208/765-7223). The **Idaho Department of Parks and Recreation** (2885 Kathleen Ave., Coeur d'Alene, 208/769-1511) maintains its north region headquarters in Coeur d'Alene. The **Coeur d'Alene Parks Department** (710 E. Mullan Ave., Coeur d'Alene, 208/769-2252) has additional information about area recreation.

National Public Radio listeners can pick up Spokane's **KPBX** (91.1 FM). Another station, featuring a great jazz repertoire, is **KEWU** (89.5 FM), the radio station of Eastern Washington University in Cheney.

If you need emergency medical services, head to **Kootenai Medical Center** (2003 Kootenai Health Way, Coeur d'Alene, 208/666-2000) just off Lincoln Way near I-90.

GETTING THERE AND AROUND
Getting There

Spokane International Airport (GEG, 9000 W. Airport Dr., Spokane, WA, 509/455-6455) is about 35 miles away. It's served by several major airlines, including Alaska Airlines, Southwest, United, and Delta. The airport has a typical gamut of rental car agencies inside the main terminal.

Shuttle service to and from Coeur d'Alene and the surrounding area is provided by **Payless Airport Shuttle** (208/762-7433 or 888/870-7433, $45 one-way for 1–2 people) by appointment only.

Getting Around

Parking in downtown Coeur d'Alene can be challenging, especially during the peak summer months. If you don't feel like riding a bike, jump on one of the free **Citylink** (www.idahocitylink.com) buses, which have three urban routes and service to the Coeur d'Alene Casino in Worley. See the website for schedule and route information.

POST FALLS

Frederick Post planted the seed for the city of Post Falls when he built a sawmill along the Spokane River in 1800. He needed permission from the locals to take advantage of the falls for his mill, so he negotiated a land-use deal with Coeur d'Alene Chief Seltice. Today the riverfront city between Coeur d'Alene and Spokane is one of Idaho's fastest-growing towns, with a population that has more than tripled since 1980 to over 26,000.

Parks

Legend has it that Post and Chief Seltice signed their deal on **Treaty Rock,** today preserved as part of a small four-acre park near the corner of Seltice and Compton Streets, two blocks west of Spokane Street. Short trails wind through the park and lead to the historic granite outcropping. Post's name is indeed carved on the rock, and below it are some Native American pictographs. But as the interpretive information at the site notes, no concrete evidence exists that this rock is actually the "contract" between Post and Seltice.

At **Falls Park,** visitors can walk to overviews of Post's famous falls and the narrow Spokane River gorge. Interpretive signs illuminate early area history; picnic tables, a playground, and a small fishpond make the 22-acre park a pleasant place for a lunch break. To get to the park, head south on Spokane Street from I-90 and watch for a posted right turn at 4th Street.

Q'emiln Riverside Park was once the site of a Coeur d'Alene Indian village. Q'emiln (ka-MEE-lin) means "throat of the river" in the Coeur d'Alene language. This 90-acre park on the south side of the Spokane River has five miles of beautiful hiking trails through steep, rocky gorges. Also here are boat ramps, horseshoe pits, playground areas, and picnic shelters. A parking fee ($3.50 cars/$6 boats) is charged Memorial Day–Labor Day. To get to the park, take I-90 Exit 5 for Spokane Street, follow Spokane Street south across the river, and turn right on Park Way Drive just on the other side.

Corbin Park is named for early Post Falls railroad developer D. C. Corbin. The 24-acre park lies on the riverbank on the west side of town and offers a softball diamond, a volleyball court, a boat ramp, and picnic areas. To get here, take I-90 Exit 2 for Pleasant View Avenue and head south to Riverbend Avenue; take Riverbend east (left) to Corbin Park Road, and follow it into the park.

For more information on the city's parks, contact **Post Falls Parks and Recreation** (408 Spokane St., Post Falls, 208/773-0539).

Centennial Trail

From Post Falls, you can follow the Centennial Trail bike and hiking path all the way to Higgins Point on Coeur d'Alene Lake, or west to Spokane and beyond. The 63-mile-long interstate trail system is a favorite of hikers, cyclists, and skaters in summer and cross-country skiers in winter. Access the trail at Falls Park.

Cruises

The **Red Lion River Queen** (208/773-1611) sternwheeler cruises up the Spokane River on sightseeing excursions in summer. The 90-minute cruises ($16.75 ages 13–54, $12 ages 4–12, $15.75 over age 54) depart Red Lion Templin's Hotel on the river at 2 P.M. Tuesday–Friday and at 11 A.M. Saturday. They also offer Sunday brunch cruises, wine-tasting cruises, and various seasonal cruises.

Boating

Rent a boat for fishing or cruising the Spokane River or Coeur d'Alene Lake at **Red Lion**

Templin's Hotel on the River (414 E. 1st Ave., Post Falls, 208/773-1611). The hotel's marina rents out gas-powered pontoon boats for $75–95 an hour, with a two-hour minimum.

Rock Climbing

The city's **Q'emiln Riverside Park** offers dozens of single-pitch bolted climbs on reasonably solid river-canyon granite. It's a beautiful spot and seldom gets crowded. If you drive into the park, you'll have to pay a parking fee. Climbers being climbers, most park just outside the gate on Park Way Drive and walk in; from the entrance gate it's just a short hike to the climbing areas.

Accommodations

Sleep Inn (157 Pleasant View Rd., Post Falls, off I-90 Exit 2, 208/777-9394 or 800/851-3178, from $99 d) and **Howard Johnson Express Inn** (3647 W. 5th Ave., Post Falls, 208/773-4541 or 800/829-3124, from $60) each offer an indoor pool, a hot tub, and free continental breakfast. On the east side of town, **Comfort Inn** (3175 E. Seltice Way, Post Falls, 208/773-8900 or 800/424-6423, from $92 d) offers 47 guest rooms and a complimentary continental breakfast bar.

Red Lion Templin's Hotel on the River (414 E. 1st Ave., Post Falls, 208/773-1611 or 800/283-6754, www.redlion.com, from $149 d) sits on the banks of the Spokane River and is the state's only hotel listed in *Idaho Wildlife Viewing Guide* as an outstanding critter-watching site. Ospreys and mallard ducks are among the hotel's neighbors. Amenities include an indoor pool, a sauna, a spa, a fitness center, tennis courts, a marina with boat rentals, guest laundry, and a restaurant overlooking the river. Nonsmoking and wheelchair-accessible rooms are available, as are suites with jetted tubs, family suites, and parlor suites.

The River Cove B&B (212 Parkwood Pl., Post Falls, 208/773-1014, www.therivercove.com, from $129) bills itself as "a scenic waterfront retreat." From the back deck you can look past the pines to the water's edge below. Each of the guest rooms has a private bath, and rates include a gourmet breakfast. In winter, you can enjoy cross-country skiing right on the premises. Smoking is allowed outside only, and small children are not allowed.

RV Parks

RVers in the area have two good options to park their rigs for the night. **Coeur d'Alene RV Resort** (2652 E. Mullan Ave., Post Falls, 208/773-3527, around $35) is an upscale park offering 191 spotless sites with full hookups. Amenities include a beautiful clubhouse with a fireplace; a heated pool, spa, and fitness center; a playground; tennis and volleyball courts; horseshoe pits; and a nine-hole putting green.

Suntree RV Park (350 N. Idahline Rd., Post Falls, 208/777-8888, www.suntreervpark. com, $34–38) offers 111 sites with full hookups. Amenities include a pool, a hot tub, and shower and laundry facilities.

Food

One of the region's best restaurants lies outside Post Falls in sleepy little Hauser Lake, a short and scenic drive away. At **(Chef in the Forest** (12008 N. Woodland Beach Dr., Post Falls, 208/773-3654, www.chefintheforest.net, from 5:30 P.M. Wed.–Thurs. and Sat., from 5 P.M. Fri. and Sun., entrées $21–36) the dinner-only menu features appetizers like warm Brie with fresh fruit and entrées such as roast duckling with fresh brandied raspberry sauce and filet mignon forestière covered with sautéed mushrooms. Great food, wine, and atmosphere make this a favorite excursion for area residents. Reservations are strongly recommended. From Post Falls, take Seltice west to McGuire Road, McGuire north to Highway 53, then west to Hauser Lake Road, and go east on North Woodland Beach Drive around the lake to the restaurant.

In town, the **White House Grill** (712 N. Spokane St., Post Falls, 208/777-9672, www. whitehousegrill.com, lunch and dinner Mon.–Sat., $8–16) dishes up Greek food with a whole lot of attitude. The employees are zany at this little restaurant, which serves everything from deep-fried feta and hummus to gyro sandwiches and lamb kebobs. Let's not forget flaky baklava and retsina wine.

WOLF LODGE DISTRICT
Eagle-Watching

A short distance east of Coeur d'Alene on I-90, Exit 22 is marked "Wolf Lodge District," where Wolf Lodge Creek empties into Wolf Lodge Bay. Wolves are no longer in evidence, but the bay's kokanee salmon population attracts a sizable population of bald eagles each winter. The eagles migrate down from the Canadian northlands to escape the harsh arctic winter. Here they find a relatively mild climate and easy food—the kokanee congregate to spawn and die at just about the same time the eagles begin arriving in late November. The eagle population peaks in late December—about 40 birds on average—and by March most of them have moved on. The best viewing time is in early morning, when the eagles do most of their feeding. The best viewing locations are at the Mineral Ridge Boat Ramp on the south side of the bay and at the Mineral Ridge trailhead, a little farther down the road on Beauty Bay.

Hiking

The **Mineral Ridge National Recreation Trail** leaves from the Mineral Ridge Recreation Area, which you'll come to just after rounding the corner from Wolf Lodge Bay into Beauty Bay on Highway 97. The 3.3-mile nature trail loops past an abandoned mine and cabin. The **Caribou Ridge National Recreation Trail** makes a nice day hike, running 4.6 miles from Beauty Creek Campground up to the Mount Coeur d'Alene Picnic Area. You'll find huckleberries in season along the way, and there are great views of the lake. The trail is moderately difficult, climbing 1,800 vertical feet in four switchbacks up onto the ridge. Beauty Creek Campground is less than a mile down Forest Road 438, which turns off Highway 97 along the east shore of Beauty Bay.

Horseback Riding

Rider Ranch (6219 S. Wolf Lodge Creek Rd., Coeur d'Alene, 208/667-3373, www.riderranch.com) offers guided trail rides, hayrides, and parties for kids on a family-owned and operated working ranch in Wolf Lodge Creek Valley. Basic 90-minute trail rides ($40 pp) have a two-person minimum. Chuck wagon dinner rides ($55 pp) have a six-person minimum. All activities are scheduled by advance reservation only. Wolf Lodge Creek Road turns off the frontage road on the north side of I-90, a little less than a mile east of Exit 22.

Accommodations

You'll find the ultimate in solitude at **Wolf Lodge Creek B&B** (515 S. Wolf Lodge Creek Rd., Coeur d'Alene, 208/667-5902 or 800/919-9653, www.wolflodge.com, $125–250). Deer graze alongside the horses in this tranquil valley. You can hear yourself think out here, yet you're less than a half-hour's drive from the city. The big and modern wooden bed-and-breakfast sits on 27 acres and has five guest rooms, all with private baths. A separate cabin is also available. Hiking opportunities are right outside the door—the inn adjoins national forest lands—and a hot tub and sauna provide great evening relaxation. Rates include a full country breakfast.

Camping

Lake Coeur d'Alene Camping Resort (10588 E. Wolf Lodge Bay Rd., Coeur d'Alene, 208/664-4471 or 888/664-4471, www.camp-cda.com) is on the south side of I-90. Among the plethora of amenities: lake access with free small-boat moorage for guests; a heated pool and spa; a playground; hiking and bike trails; laundry and shower facilities; and boat and canoe rentals. The resort has 47 RV sites ($32–43) with hookups, 48 tent sites ($27), and 19 cabins ($56–135).

Along the I-90 frontage road 1.7 miles east of the Wolf Lodge exit (north side of I-90) is **Wolf Lodge Campground** (12329 E. Frontage Rd., Coeur d'Alene, 208/664-2812). The RV park offers 55 grassy sites ($30–35) with hookups on a large pleasant flat along Wolf Lodge Creek. Tent sites ($22) and cabins ($50–115) are also available.

Also in the area is the U.S. Forest Service **Beauty Creek Campground** (20 sites, $18), just up Road 438 from Beauty Bay.

Food

Folks come from miles around for the steaks at **Wolf Lodge Inn** (11741 E. Frontage Rd., Coeur d'Alene, 208/664-6665, dinner daily). Here you can get darn near half a steer served up in front of you; the Rancher cut weighs in at 42 ounces. All steaks are flame-broiled over an open-pit cherrywood and tamarack fire and served with salad, bread, and buckaroo beans. Also on the menu are shrimp, salmon, trout, lamb chops, scallops, and, yes, Rocky Mountain oysters. Reservations are recommended.

LAKE COEUR D'ALENE SCENIC BYWAY

If you continue south from the Wolf Lodge exit around the east shore of the lake, you'll be traveling on the state's designated Lake Coeur d'Alene Scenic Byway. Keep your eyes peeled for ospreys; this area has the largest concentration of them in the western United States. The beautiful birds love the wetlands around the lake's east shore. You won't have to look so hard to spot the sunsets around here—the showy spectacles light up the sky and lake on a regular basis.

Arrow Point

About nine miles south of Beauty Bay en route to Harrison is the **Arrow Point Resort** (4502 S. Arrow Point Rd., Harrison, 877/525-3232, www.arrowpointresort.com, around $200), which occupies a finger of land jutting into the lake. The secluded, upscale resort offers furnished 2–3-bedroom condo units, a marina, beaches, and an indoor pool.

Bell Bay

At the south end of Powderhorn Bay, Highway 97 turns inland briefly before crossing the Coeur d'Alene River and rolling into Harrison. This inland stretch cuts off the nose of a peninsula sticking out into the lake. Here Road 314 (E. Point Rd.) turns off the highway and leads west some three miles across wide-open private

BOUNTIFUL BIKE TRAILS

Over the past few years, north Idaho has become one of the best bicycling destinations anywhere, thanks to the Route of the Hiawatha and the Trail of the Coeur d'Alenes, two unforgettable biking experiences.

The 15-mile **Route of the Hiawatha** is a rails-to-trails conversion on the old Milwaukee Road. The main trailhead (accessible via I-90 Exit 5 at Taft, Montana) begins just outside the 8,771-foot St. Paul Pass Tunnel, which means you start and end your ride by cycling through the 1.8-mile tunnel — in the dark, with only a bike light or headlamp to guide you. The packed gravel trail includes eight other tunnels and seven railway trestles, the highest 230 feet off the valley floor. Guardrails and a gentle downhill grade make the Route of the Hiawatha an easy and enjoyable ride for nearly everyone. A shuttle ($9 adults, $6 ages 6-13) runs from the end of the trail back to the first tunnel several times each day late May-early October.

Bike rentals, including lights and a rack, and trail passes ($9 adults, $6 ages 6-13) are available at the trailhead and at Lookout Pass ski area (I-90 Exit 0 on the Montana-Idaho border east of Wallace, 208/744-1301, www.skilookout.com).

The **Trail of the Coeur d'Alenes,** now an Idaho state park, spans 72 miles across the Idaho Panhandle from Mullan in the east to Plummer in the west. The fully paved trail sits on the old Union Pacific rail bed and marks the railroad's efforts — in conjunction with the state of Idaho and the Coeur d'Alene Tribe, which comanages the trail — to seal over the mine waste and tailings that contaminated the area in its mining heyday. Signs along the way warn users to stay on the trail and eat at designated waysides, which may make some cyclists feel squeamish about riding the trail at all, but state and tribal officials say casual users need not worry about contamination.

The best and most scenic part of the mostly flat, free-access trail lies between Pinehurst (milepost 48.7), where it leaves the I-90 corridor, and the old Chatcolet Bridge south of Harrison (near milepost 8). Avid cyclists may want to tackle this section in a long day, but most riders will want to savor shorter out-and-back rides that can be done along any stretch of it. Be sure to carry your own water and snacks, since services are limited in most areas. Remember, though, that you can get a filling meal at the Enaville Resort near milepost 47, and an enormous ice cream cone at The Creamery in Harrison (milepost 15).

Bike rentals and shuttle service are available at **Excelsior Cycle & Sport Shop** (21 Railroad Ave., Kellogg, 208/786-3751) and **Pedal Pushers** (101 N. Coeur d'Alene Ave., Harrison, 208/689-3436). Maps and brochures are available at all trailheads, or contact the trail office at **Old Mission State Park** (31732 S. Mission Rd., Cataldo, 208/682-3814).

property to the U.S. Forest Service **Bell Bay Campground** (26 sites, $14–16) on the lakeshore. You'll feel isolated out here—it's a nice place to kick back.

Harrison

Until 1889 the southeast shore of Coeur d'Alene Lake was part of the Coeur d'Alene Indian Reservation, but then timber companies cruising the area decided that the shore would be a perfect spot for a sawmill, so they planted a bug in then-president Benjamin Harrison's ear. Harrison "withdrew" a narrow strip of land from the reservation to accommodate the loggers.

The town was founded in 1891 and named after the president to ensure greasy wheels for the future. By the turn of the century, Harrison was home to 2,000 people, 11 lumber mills, a dozen saloons, and a thriving red-light district. Steamboats plying Coeur d'Alene Lake made Harrison a major port of call, and at one point it was the largest population center on the lake. But fire devastated the town in 1917, and shortly thereafter the arrival of railroads rendered the steamboats obsolete. The local timber industry dwindled, and Harrison's glory days were over.

Today the town's 270-some residents rely on tourism to feed the coffers. Fishing and boating were long the primary draws, but increasing numbers of cyclists are using Harrison as a base camp for the Trail of the Coeur d'Alenes. Sunsets are stupendous here too. If you're looking for a refuge from the hectic tourist scene on the north shore of the lake, Harrison offers it.

If you're here to ride, **Pedal Pushers** (101 N. Coeur d'Alene Ave., Harrison, 208/689-3436, www.bikenorthidaho.com) is the place to get bike gear and other information. The shop rents bikes (road bikes $9 per hour, 2-hour minimum) and related equipment like car racks and helmets. It also offers repairs and runs seasonal shuttle service for the Trail of the Coeur d'Alenes.

Cyclists and other travelers congregate at the **Osprey Inn** (134 Frederick Ave., Harrison, 208/689-9502, www.ospreyinn.com, $66–120). Built in 1915, the inn was originally a boardinghouse for lumberjacks. Each of the five newly reconstructed guest rooms has a private bath with a shower. Rates include full breakfast. Harrison also offers RV and tent camping at its waterfront, with a small swimming beach and playground nearby.

Harrison's big annual event is the **Old Time Picnic,** held on the last weekend in July. In addition to potato salad and hot dogs, look for live entertainment and a parade along the lake. For more information, visit the **Harrison Chamber of Commerce** (www.harrisonidaho.org).

Chain of Lakes Route

South of Harrison, Highway 97 runs into a T intersection with Highway 3. If you turn right, you'll end up in St. Maries. Turn left to stay on the designated scenic byway, which takes you up the South Fork Coeur d'Alene River past 10 major lakes. Most of the wetlands in this Chain of Lakes area are included in the **Coeur d'Alene River Wildlife Management Area,** a favorite stopover for migratory waterfowl.

This beautiful area harbors a dirty little secret. Each spring, tundra swans stop at the Chain of Lakes on their way south; many never make it out. The area lies downstream from the Kellogg Superfund site, and the aquatic plants here contain deadly concentrations of lead. The swans eat the contaminated plants and die of starvation as the lead and other heavy metals inhibit nutrient absorption. Local environmentalists morbidly dub the annual event "The Rite of Spring." As you drive up this scenic highway, eventually rejoining I-90 near Cataldo, it's hard to imagine environmental problems lurking unseen. For more information, call the Idaho Department of Fish and Game's Coeur d'Alene office (208/769-1414).

The Silver Valley

East of Coeur d'Alene, I-90 climbs Fourth of July Pass and drops down the other side into the valley of the South Fork Coeur d'Alene River. In 1859, Jesuit missionary Pierre Jean de Smet described this valley as a verdant paradise: "Imagine thick, untrodden forest, strewn with thousands of trees thrown down by age and storms in every direction, where the path is scarcely visible." But this almost primeval scene was not to last. In 1885, prospector Noah Kellogg discovered a huge vein of a lead-silver-zinc ore called galena near the present-day town of Wardner. The find brought miners and mining companies flooding into the area, burrowing into the hills like mad, money-hungry moles. Over the next 100 years, more than $5 billion in precious metals would be taken from the earth, making "The Silver Valley" one of the most lucrative mining districts in world history while at the same time turning it into a lifeless toxic waste dump. The once verdant forests of the South

Fork were cut down for houses, mine timbers, and railroad ties. But that was just the beginning. In 1917 the first lead smelter was built near the Bunker Hill mine so that ore could be processed on-site. The U.S. Environmental Protection Agency's Superfund site description tersely outlines the consequences:

> During the majority of time the smelters were operating, few environmental protection procedures or controls were used. As a result, there is widespread contamination of soil, water, and air from lead and other heavy metals.

The smelters belched toxic plumes into the air, and the sulfur dioxide fallout killed what vegetation was left on the hillside. Water pollution was an even greater problem. Until 1938, all residues from the Bunker Hill's mine tailings were discharged directly into the Coeur d'Alene River. Thereafter, the wastes were diverted into an unlined settling pond that leaked toxic effluent into the groundwater. In addition, spring floods routinely washed heavy metals from tailings piles into the river and on downstream. Between the 1880s and the 1960s, an estimated 72 million tons of contaminated tailings ended up in the Coeur d'Alene River system; today scientists debate the potential health threat of the heavy-metal sludge coating the bottom of Coeur d'Alene Lake.

Meanwhile, in the mid-1970s, it was discovered that lead had found its way into the blood of the valley's children in alarming concentrations. A class-action suit brought by a number of parents against Gulf Resources and Chemical Corporation, then-owner of the Bunker Hill mine, ended in an out-of-court settlement, but the lead problem persists, as evidenced by the Panhandle Health District's publication *Coeur d'Alene River System and Heavy Metal Exposure, A Public Awareness Message*. Among other precautions, the pamphlet advises local residents:

> Clean shoes and change soil-stained clothes before going home. Keep soiled clothing in a plastic bag and launder it separate from the rest of your wash. Don't can whole fish caught from the lower Coeur d'Alene River system. Don't eat large amounts of fish, water fowl, or aquatic plants.

The Bunker Hill smelters shut down in 1981, pulling the rug out from under the local economy and leaving behind one of the country's largest Superfund toxic-cleanup sites. A 1992 report by the U.S. Geological Survey called the Coeur d'Alene River drainage the worst example of heavy-metal pollution in the world. Gulf conveniently declared bankruptcy, sticking taxpayers with the cleanup tab.

The towering smokestacks of the Bunker Hill smelters—built in 1977 in an attempt to disperse toxic clouds away from the local citizenry—were demolished in May 1996, and the blood-lead levels of valley residents today have declined to just above normal. The ongoing Superfund cleanup is making progress on a 21-square-mile area around Kellogg, and the hillsides are recovering their natural blanket of green. But heavy metals continue to leach into the river from upstream mine sites, flowing down to Coeur d'Alene Lake and into Washington.

Small-scale mining still takes place in the Kellogg area today, but the valley has turned to tourism as a long-term solution for generating revenue. In 1988, Kellogg's citizens voted to tax themselves in order to spruce up the local ski hill and install the world's longest gondola to get people here. Today, Silver Mountain Resort is the town's biggest draw in both winter and summer.

FOURTH OF JULY PASS

East of Wolf Lodge Bay, I-90 ascends and crests Fourth of July Pass (3,070 feet). The pass gets its name from an Independence Day weekend celebrated in 1861 by U.S. Army engineer Lieutenant John Mullan (1830–1909) and his crew of road builders. They were working on what later became known as the **Mullan Road,** a historic route connecting Fort

Benton, Montana, with Fort Walla Walla, Washington.

Originally intended as a military road and an alternative to south Idaho's Oregon Trail, the route came to be used by railroad builders and miners in the Coeur d'Alene River valley. Today, I-90 overlays much of Mullan's old road.

I-90 Exit 28, atop the pass, leads to two sites of interest. On the north side of the highway is **Mullan Road Historical Park,** where a 0.5-mile interpretive trail leads to the Mullan Tree, or rather the place where the Mullan Tree once grew. It had been engraved with the words "M. R., July 4, 1861." The "M. R." probably stood for "Military Road," not "Mullan Road." But consensus has it that John Mullan was an intelligent and resourceful man, so what the heck, Mullan Road it is. In any case, the western white pine blew down in 1962, and Mullan's inscription was removed for preservation and is on display at the Museum of North Idaho in Coeur d'Alene. The site is a little anticlimactic as a result, but the path through the woods is delightful. In the parking lot is a monumental bust of Mullan whose face, unfortunately, has fallen off.

On the south side of the highway is **Fourth of July Pass Park N' Ski Area.** A large parking area provides access to two five-mile loop trails and a third nonlooping trail that continues through the woods for just under two miles. Some steep grades on the loops make those trails best suited to intermediate or better skiers. The third trail is gentle enough for beginners.

CATALDO AND VICINITY
◖ Old Mission State Park

Old Mission State Park (31732 S. Mission Rd., Cataldo, 208/682-3814, 8 A.M.–6 P.M. daily summer, 9 A.M.–5 P.M. daily in other seasons, parking $5) is at I-90 Exit 39. Even from a distance the old Cataldo mission, visible from I-90, is powerful and striking. At once monumental and simple, the Greek Revival–style structure sits atop a grassy hill that slopes down to the placid waters of the

the old Cataldo mission

© IDAHO DIVISION OF TOURISM

South Fork of the Coeur d'Alene River. It fits naturally into its surroundings, a tribute to the man who designed and helped build the mission and served as its first spiritual leader, Father Antonio Ravalli, born May 16, 1812, in Ferrara, Italy. Ravalli was ordained as a Jesuit priest in 1843 and sent to work with the Coeur d'Alene Indians alongside Father Pierre Jean de Smet. When Ravalli arrived, de Smet's mission was located on the St. Joe River near present-day St. Maries, but the regular floods (a phenomenon that persists today) caused de Smet to look for a higher and drier spot. Ravalli was assigned the task of supervising the relocation.

The park's literature calls Ravalli a Renaissance man; while that might be a cliché, it fits him perfectly. By the time he reached Idaho at the age of 31, Ravalli had studied literature, philosophy, theology, mathematics, science, medicine, art, and architecture. The Native Americans and missionaries began building the mission in 1847, following Ravalli's plans, out of hand-hewn timbers held together with wooden pegs. The foot-thick walls were made of woven straw and river mud. The result, formally called the Mission of the Sacred Heart, is the oldest building still standing in Idaho.

The exterior is beautiful, but Ravalli's artistic handiwork and creativity really shine inside. Out on the wild frontier, with no budget to speak of, Ravalli became a master at decorating on the cheap. See that marble altar? It's actually made of wood, carefully painted by Ravalli to simulate marble. And those cast iron chandeliers? They're tin, cut into elegant patterns by the artistic priest. Ravalli also painted the side altars with scenes depicting heaven and hell and carved the statues of the Virgin Mary and Saint John the Evangelist standing on either side of the altar.

The mission opened for worship in 1853 and operated for 23 years. During that time it served as a welcome resting place for Native Americans, pioneers, John Mullan's road-building crew, and military contingents. Father Joseph Cataldo, a strong and popular leader of Idaho's Roman Catholics, took the reins in 1865; the nearby town is named in his honor. In 1876, mission activities were relocated to DeSmet in a political move that was heartbreaking for the mission's Native American congregation.

Today, the mission serves as the centerpiece of an outstanding state historic park. A modern interpretive center screens a short film illustrating the mission's history and offers exhibits about the Coeur d'Alene Indians and the Jesuits. Self-guided interpretive trails lead across the grounds to natural features and points of historical interest.

The park hosts a few events each year. On the second Sunday in July is the **Historic Skills Fair,** where you can watch spinning, quilting, black powder shooting, and other anachronisms done just the way the old-timers used to do. On August 15 is the annual **Coeur d'Alene Indian Pilgrimage** and its associated "Coming of the Black Robes Pageant." Traditional Native American foods are featured.

Snowcat Skiing

Peak Adventures (208/818-9408, www.peaksnowcats.com, Dec.–Apr.), at I-90 Exit 40 in Cataldo, offers snowcat ski trips high into the St. Joe Mountains south of town. The cost for full-day trips is $225, including guides and lunch; reservations are required.

UP THE NORTH FORK OF THE COEUR D'ALENE RIVER

The next town you come to as you head east from Cataldo on I-90 is Kingston, near the confluence of the two major forks of the Coeur d'Alene River. I-90 follows the South Fork, while Forest Highway 9 leaves I-90 and follows the North Fork up to the old gold-mining towns of Prichard and Murray. Besides its considerable history, the North Fork area is rife with recreation opportunities.

Note: On older Forest Service maps, the North Fork of the Coeur d'Alene is labeled as the main Coeur d'Alene River, while the Little North Fork—the first major tributary of the North Fork—is labeled the North Fork of the Coeur d'Alene. The Forest Service has changed this to reflect standard local usage on its newer maps.

Enaville Resort

Off I-90 Exit 43 and 1.5 miles north on Coeur d'Alene River Road (Forest Hwy. 9) is Enaville Resort (208/682-3453, www.enavilleresort.com, breakfast, lunch, and dinner daily). It's not a resort like the Coeur d'Alene Resort; it's more like a last resort. Enaville was established in 1880 and over the years within its log walls has been a gold rush–era bar, a railroad way station, a boardinghouse, and a whorehouse. Today it's a family restaurant and tavern specializing in such delectables as buffalo burgers and Rocky Mountain oysters. Kitschy Western art and memorabilia—including old swords and a blunderbuss—fill the walls, floors, and ceilings. It's all a bit of living history and definitely worth a stop for a meal.

The Little North Fork

Little North Fork Road leads up to the U.S.

Forest Service **Bumblebee Campground** (25 sites, $16) and, after another 20 miles or so to **Honeysuckle Campground** (8 sites, $16). Between the two campgrounds is Laverne Creek, which marks a boundary for anglers. From here on upriver, fishing is catch-and-release only with single barbless hooks, flies and lures only, and no bait. The Little North Fork is stocked with rainbows above Bumblebee Campground.

Prichard

Twenty-three miles from Kingston is Prichard, a town named after the first prospector to strike gold in the Coeur d'Alenes. Today there's not a whole lot here, but Silver Valley residents come from miles around for the prime rib dinners at **Gloria's Steak House & Lodge** (21428 Coeur d'Alene River Rd., 208/682-3031, daily year-round). Gloria's also rents motel rooms ($50–100; rates include prime rib dinner for two) and has a hot tub.

To Murray

At Prichard, you can turn off the North Fork and head east up Prichard Creek. At the confluence of Prichard and Eagle Creeks, turning up Forest Road 152, then Forest Road 805, leads up the west fork of Eagle Creek to **Settlers Grove of Ancient Cedars.** A trail winds through the grove, which has many trees 6–8 feet in diameter.

Continuing east on Prichard Creek Road, you'll soon come to the gold-rush boomtown of Murray. As many as 25,000 people lived in the area between Murray and neighboring Eagle City in its heyday. Wyatt Earp ran a saloon in Eagle in the 1880s, and Murray was the Shoshone County seat for 14 years. You'd never guess it looking at the sleepy little town today. You can thank the Coeur d'Alene Mining Company, which dredged Prichard Creek 1917–1924, for the ugly tailings piles along the creek-side.

More area history can be gleaned at **The Sprag Pole** (6353 Prichard Creek Rd., Murray, 208/682-3901), which consists of a friendly bar and grill on one side and Walt's Museum, a

veritable warehouse full of great old stuff, on the other. A sprag pole was the old-time equivalent of a parking brake—a long pole strategically planted to keep wagons from rolling. The other bar in town is the **Bedroom Goldmine Bar** (6273 Prichard Creek Rd., Murray, 208/682-4394), site of the Bedroom Mine. A former owner sunk a shaft right in his bedroom. It's no longer being used.

From Murray, you can head back to Kingston the way you came, or take Forest Road 456 over King's and Dobson Passes 20 miles to Wallace. The old **Murray Cemetery,** at the bottom of King's Pass grade on the way out of town toward Wallace, has the graves of such famous locals as Andrew Prichard and Maggie Hall, a kindly madam better known as Molly B'Damn.

KELLOGG AND VICINITY

In attempting to rise anew from the ashes of its mining industry, Kellogg took two major steps: It replaced the narrow winding road up to the local ski hill with the world's longest gondola, which now whisks skiers up some 3,400 vertical feet in 3.1 miles to the snowy slopes; and it gave the town a partial face-lift, turning it into a Bavarian-themed village. The gondola might be called a success—it's certainly a unique attraction and makes it easier for visitors to enjoy the mountain. The Alpine Village, however, seems a little out of place. Other than snowy peaks, nothing about this gritty mining town or the surrounding area is even vaguely reminiscent of the Alps. Uptown Kellogg is a charming historic district, but many of the storefronts sit vacant as all the attention is given to the area surrounding the burgeoning Silver Mountain Resort.

Silver Mountain

There has been a ski area on the slopes of Kellogg and Wardner Peaks since the late 1960s. First called Jackass (for Noah Kellogg's famous donkey), then Silverhorn, the resort struggled with one main drawback: the steep, circuitous road skiers needed to negotiate to reach the base area from Kellogg. When the

© IDAHO DIVISION OF TOURISM

skiing at Silver Mountain near Kellogg

mines shut down in the early 1980s, Silver Mountain represented the city's best hope for economic recovery—a chance to fill the void with tourist dollars. The late city councilman Wayne Ross envisioned an aerial tramway that would bypass the road and take visitors directly from town to the mountaintop. He successfully negotiated funding, and in 1990 the new, improved **Silver Mountain Ski Resort** (610 Bunker Ave., Kellogg, at I-90 Exit 49, 208/783-1111 or 866/344-2675, www.silvermt. com, 9 A.M.–4 P.M. daily, lift tickets $50 ages 18–61, $35 ages 7–17, $40 over age 61, free under age 7) with the world's longest single-stage gondola (3.1 miles) opened.

The area gets plenty of snow—some 300 inches per year on average. The resort has 1,500 acres with a 2,200-foot vertical drop and a longest run of 2.5 miles. Intermediate runs are most prevalent, but 40 percent of the runs are either advanced or expert. Besides the gondola, the area is served by one fixed-grip quad, two triple chairs, two double chairs, and a surface lift. The gondolas also take people

up to the four-lane tubing hill (Sat.–Sun. and holidays, $20 adults, $18 youth and seniors) for two-hour sessions. Scenic gondola rides (17 adults, $13 youth and seniors) are possible year-round.

In summer, the resort is open weekends and holidays only and hosts barbecues and entertainment in its mountaintop amphitheater. Other summertime draws include gondola-served hiking and mountain biking on an extensive, newly expanded trail system. A single ride up the gondola in summer costs $17 adults, $13 juniors; family rates are available. Full-day mountain-bike passes also are available.

The resort recently unveiled an indoor water park connected to its fancy new lodge. **Silver Rapids Water Park** is an expansive year-round aqua playground featuring a continuous surf wave, a flowing river, waterslides, private cabanas, and a small restaurant with hot tubs, but you must be a guest of the resort's Morning Star Lodge. Packages start at $199 for four people, which includes a studio suite in the lodge and a two-day pass to the water park. Day-use for nonguests can be arranged for parties of 15 or more.

Bunker Hill Staff House Museum

Otherwise known as the Shoshone County Mining and Smelting Museum, this museum (820 McKinley Ave., Kellogg, 208/786-4141, 10 A.M.–6 P.M. daily late May–Sept., small entrance fee) occupies the former staff house for resident and visiting bigwigs of the Bunker Hill & Sullivan Mine Co. The house was built in 1906 for a manager of the Bunker Hill mine. Exhibits cover the town's mining history, with an emphasis on Bunker Hill itself. A great collection of old photos includes one of a burro, supposedly Noah Kellogg's famous sidekick. Another display lists the Bunker Hill's staggering statistics: 1,900 tons of ore mined daily; 400 tons of waste rock removed daily; 3,500 gallons of water expelled per minute; 160,000 cubic feet of air circulated each minute. During the mine's 96-year life span, 37 million tons of ore were excavated, yielding more than 165 million ounces of silver, as well as copious amounts of lead and zinc. Don't miss the display in the basement—an ingenious 3-D model of the Bunker Hill mine's enormous underground labyrinth.

Wardner

To see where it all began, take Kellogg's Division Street up the hill into Milo Gulch to the town of Wardner (population 230). Just 1,000 yards up the gulch from today's Wardner City Hall, Noah Kellogg found the gleaming rock that sparked the Silver Valley's mining boom. In "downtown" Wardner, locals keep the memories of the mining days alive at **Wardner Gift Shop and Museum** (652 Main St., 208/786-2641). The free museum has a fascinating collection of photographs and memorabilia.

Noah Kellogg's Grave

On the way up Division Street heading toward Wardner, you'll spot signs directing you east (left) up the flanks of the mountain to the local cemetery. Here you'll find the grave of Noah Kellogg, marked by a fence and a tasteless modern monument that steals all dignity from the site. It's a poignant place to ponder the dead miners who couldn't take their wealth with them, and the costs of their obsession on the scarred valley below.

Sunshine Mine Memorial

The Sunshine Mine is recognized as the world's all-time greatest silver producer. But on May 2, 1972, extraction of that bounty exacted a horrific price. Some time after 11 A.M. a fire broke out more than 3,000 feet down in the mine's depths. Warnings spread as soon as the first smoke was noticed. Those among the 173 miners at work that day who got word of the blaze bolted for the hoists that would take them toward the surface. Failure of a mine-wide alarm system prevented others from getting the warning until it was too late. Smoke and carbon monoxide soon asphyxiated the hoist operators, trapping the miners left beneath them. Despite the valiant efforts of local, national, and even international rescue workers, 91 miners died in the tragedy. Just east of Kellogg, off I-90 Exit 54, is the Sunshine Mine Memorial, a huge sculpture of a miner at work dedicated to those who died in the disaster.

Accommodations

On the low-priced end of the spectrum are **Sunshine Inn** (301 W. Cameron Ave., Kellogg, 208/784-1186), with a small restaurant and a big lounge with pool tables, and the **Trail Motel** (206 W. Cameron Ave., Kellogg, 208/784-1161, from $45 d). Both are on the north side of I-90.

GuestHouse Inn & Suites (601 Bunker Ave., Kellogg, 208/783-1234 or 800/214-8378, from $89 d) is especially noteworthy for its convenient location adjacent to the Silver Mountain gondola. Amenities at the newish 61-room hotel include an indoor pool and spa, free continental breakfast, cable TV with HBO, a guest laundry, and ski and bike storage.

One of the bigger, fancier motels in town is **◖ Silverhorn Motor Inn** (699 W. Cameron Ave., Kellogg, 208/783-1151 or 800/437-6437, www.silverhornmotorinn.com, from $89 d). It offers queen beds and an on-site restaurant, guest laundry, and a jetted tub. Pets are allowed.

Silver Mountain Resort's new **Morning Star Lodge** (610 Bunker Ave., Kellogg, 208/783-1111 or 866/344-2675, www.silvermt.com, from $199 peak season) offers plush condo-style suites ranging from studio units to lavish loft suites. The resort has several skiing and water-park packages as well as cheaper off-season rates. Amenities include kitchens, decks, and preferential treatment at the resort's facilities.

Food and Drink

Down at the gondola base, **Noah's Canteen** (610 Bunker Ave., Kellogg, 208/783-2440, lunch and dinner daily, entrées $10–27) serves upscale pub fare in a casual dining room with a roaring fireplace. Expect to find steaks, seafood, burgers, wraps, and pizza. The adjacent lounge area has more than 10 microbrews on tap.

◖ Silver Spoon Restaurant (699 W. Cameron Ave., Kellogg, 208/783-1151, 6 A.M.–9 P.M. daily, under $10), at the Silverhorn Motor Inn, offers freshly baked goods, huckleberry pancakes, and other home-spun fare.

In Uptown Kellogg, you'll find **Moose Creek Grill** (12 Emerson Lane, Kellogg, 208/783-2625, www.moosecreekgrill.com, lunch Wed.–Fri. summer, dinner Tues.–Sat. year-round, $9–25) in an old blue house. This casual new restaurant serves burgers, steaks, salads, pork chops, fish tacos, and inventive pasta dishes. Try the delish dark chocolate turtle cake for dessert. Lots of Northwestern microbrews and wines by the glass are available.

Information
The **Historic Silver Valley Chamber of Commerce** operates a visitors center (10 Station Ave., Kellogg, 208/784-0821, www.silvervalleychamber.com), which has lots of brochures and general information about the area.

◖ WALLACE
East of Kellogg, I-90 climbs through Osburn to Wallace. Of all the towns in the Silver Valley, Wallace feels most like the quintessential mining town. It is a compact place—the valley narrows into a tight canyon, forcing the town to creep off the canyon floor and up the steep wooded slopes. In the small downtown, you'll still find a mining supply store along with many well-preserved 19th-century buildings; the entire town is listed on the National Register of Historic Places. You'll discover a treasure trove of antiques shops, old saloons, funky restaurants, and museums.

Up on the hill—hidden in the trees up steep, narrow, switchbacking lanes—are old miners' cabins and newer facsimiles. This is where Hollywood starlet Lana Turner spent her early years, in a house overlooking the rough-and-tumble town.

Sometimes after a storm, when mists hang over the hillsides and raindrops drip off the rooftops and pines, the town takes on an

Wallace has a checkered past.

almost tangible tranquility. Walk up the hill—up the rickety wooden stairs, past the small clapboard houses—and you'll half expect to find a grizzled old prospector sitting on his front porch, plucking the melancholy strains of "My Darling Clementine" on a banjo. It's almost enough to make you want to trade in the minivan for a pickax and mule.

Museums

A trio of museums commemorate Wallace's three greatest industries. The **Wallace District Mining Museum** (509 Bank St., Wallace, 208/556-1592, 10 A.M.–5 P.M. daily May–Labor Day weekend, 10 A.M.–5 P.M. Mon.–Sat., 10 A.M.–3 P.M. Sun. Apr. and Sept.–Oct., 10 A.M.–5 P.M. Mon.–Fri., 10 A.M.–3 P.M. Sat.–Sun. Nov.–Mar., $3 adults, $1 ages 6–17, $7 family) offers exhibits about mining, miners, and the hard-rock life they led during the valley's boom days. You can ponder historic photos and artifacts and watch two different videos on the valley's mining history. More than 1 billion ounces of silver were mined in the region over the course of a century. That's 62.5 million pounds, or 31,250 tons.

The **Northern Pacific Depot Railroad Museum** (6th and Pine St., Wallace, 208/752-0111, 9 A.M.–7 P.M. daily summer, reduced hours spring and fall, closed Oct. 31–Mar. 15, $2 adults, $1.50 over age 59, $1 ages 6–16, $6 family) occupies the beautiful château-style 1901 Northern Pacific Depot. Bricks used in the building's construction were imported from China and destined for a fancy Tacoma hotel; the hotel never got off the ground, and the bricks ended up here. Until 1980, the Northern Pacific's Yellowstone Park Line stopped at this depot on its run between Chicago and Seattle. In 1986 the depot was carefully moved to its present site after the new I-90 threatened to run right over it. Old railroad photos and paraphernalia fill the museum. One of the most interesting exhibits is a huge glass route map that once hung in another Northern Pacific depot.

Perhaps the most interesting of the three museums is the **Oasis Bordello Museum** (605 Cedar St., Wallace, 208/753-0801, 9:30 A.M.–6:30 P.M. Mon.–Sat., 10 A.M.–5 P.M. Sun. May–early Oct., tour $5). Mining towns have historically been populated with a far higher percentage of men than women, and this imbalance created numerous business opportunities for enterprising women of questionable virtue. The Oasis was just one of several brothels that once lined this end of town. Interestingly enough, the Oasis remained in business until 1988, which was 15 years after Idaho's governor officially proclaimed prostitution illegal in the state and 93 years after the first brothel opened. The workers apparently left in a hurry, and the rooms have been preserved as they were when abandoned.

The 20-minute upstairs tour offers many interesting anecdotes, such as the fact that in 1982 the Oasis women bought the town a new police car with money saved from their earnings. Their relatively recent departure takes this museum out of the realm of a charming Western anachronism and into the somewhat seedier reality of the modern world. Nothing on the tour is particularly graphic or offensive, but it's nevertheless more jeans and G-strings than petticoats and lace. Entry is free to the ground-floor store, which sells assorted scents and frillies, and to the basement museum, which offers glimpses of a still and other artifacts from Wallace's rowdy days gone by.

Sierra Silver Mine Tour

Rarely can someone not drawing a paycheck from a mining company go down the shafts for a look around. The 75-minute Sierra Silver Mine Tour (420 5th St., Wallace, 208/752-5151, www.silverminetour.org, every 30 minutes 10 A.M.–4 P.M. daily May–early Oct., $12.50 adults, $11 seniors, $8.50 ages 4–16, $41 family of 2 adults with 2 or more kids) allows you to do just that. The mine you'll explore was once an operating silver mine. From Wallace, you'll board a trolley for the short ride to the mine, then don hard hats and make your way down into the cool, dark depths. Guides explain the mining process, history, and various techniques.

Recreation

The Route of the Hiawatha mountain bike trail goes right through Wallace along its 15-mile run to the Montana border. In summer, this brings to town an endless flow of Lycra-clad bicyclists who mingle with leather-clad Harley riders at the sidewalk cafés.

For information on the local backcountry and trail maps for the areas on both the North and South Forks of the Coeur d'Alene River, contact the U.S. Forest Service **Coeur d'Alene River Ranger District Silver Valley Office** (Smelterville, 208/783-2363).

Entertainment

Sixth Street Melodrama (212 6th St., Wallace, 208/752-8871 or 877/749-8478, www.sixthstreetmelodrama.com, $13–15) is a long-running local thespian troupe. In summer, the players present old-fashioned melodrama with plenty of audience participation. In winter and spring, the company offers more serious performances, often musicals. Check the website for a current playbill and schedule.

Events

The second Saturday in May, Wallace celebrates **Depot Days** with a street fair, a car show, food, and live music. For more information call the Northern Pacific Depot Railroad Museum (208/752-0111). The **Huckleberry/Heritage Festival** in mid-August brings a 5K run and walk, a pancake breakfast, crafts booths, and more. The chamber of commerce (208/753-7151) can fill you in on the details.

Accommodations

The Brooks Hotel (500 Cedar St., Wallace, 208/556-1571, www.thebrookshotel.com, from $70 d) is the grande dame of the old Wallace hotels, but she's a little scruffy behind the ears. Off the lobby is a good family restaurant serving three meals a day. **Stardust Motel** (410 Pine St., Wallace, 208/752-1213, $40–80) is a retro motor inn that is hit or miss in the cleanliness department, but the place is affordable, and you could easily stumble back to your

room from the saloons thanks to the motel's close proximity to downtown.

Wallace Inn (100 Front St., Wallace, 208/752-1252 or 800/643-2386, from $129 d) is the most modern and upscale place in town. Amenities include a heated indoor pool and jetted tub, a sauna and steam rooms, and a restaurant. The inn offers a free shuttle to Lookout Pass Recreation Area.

If you're into privacy, why not rent an entire house? ◖ **The Bungalow at 214 Cedar** (214 Cedar St., Wallace, 208/512-7686) is a Victorian-era home near downtown with three bedrooms and a full kitchen. You can rent the house for $85 per night per couple, $15 for each additional person up to eight guests. You'll have to leave a $500 deposit, all of which is refundable except for a $50 cleaning fee.

The **Beale House B&B** (107 Cedar St., Wallace, 208/752-7151 or 888/752-7151, from $170) occupies a 1904 Victorian residence in a quiet residential neighborhood. The house has a long and distinguished history, well documented in a collection of old photographs available for perusal. A crackling fireplace inside and a bubbling hot tub outside combine to take the chill off those après-ski evenings. Four of the five guest rooms share baths (which often turns out to private, depending on how full the place is). Rates include full breakfast. Children and pets are not allowed.

Camping and RVing

Down by the Depot RV Park (108 Nine Mile Rd., Wallace, 208/753-7121), just across the I-90 from downtown, offers 45 sites with hookups ($25) and for tents ($18). Amenities include showers, restrooms, a laundry room, a game room, and a saloon.

Food and Drink

The **1313 Club Historic Saloon & Grill** (608 Bank St., Wallace, 208/752-9391, www.1313club.com, lunch and dinner Mon.–Sat., dinner entrées $11–22) has several sidewalk tables perfect for people-watching. The efficient service and selection of microbrews in bottles and on tap are among the best in town.

The menu is all about burgers, hot sandwiches, and deep-fried finger steaks. At night, you can get big steaks and pork chops served with garlicky mashed potatoes and grilled baguette.

Nearby is ◖ **Smoke House Barbecue & Saloon** (424 6th St., Wallace, 208/659-7539, 11 A.M.–9 P.M. daily, entrées $7–27), a historic bar that dishes up apple wood–smoked pork ribs, pulled pork sandwiches, bison, wild Alaskan salmon, and brisket. Sides include red beans and rice, coleslaw, and macaroni and cheese. Service here can be spotty, but the beer is cold and the food is good enough to make up for a little forgetfulness.

Locals call Wallace the "Center of the Universe," which might help to explain why the **Red Light Garage** (5th St. and Pine St., 208/556-0575, breakfast, lunch, and dinner daily, breakfast under $10) has a spaceship in its parking lot. This funky little restaurant and junk store, in a former service station, serves burgers, burritos, wraps, and a damn good huckleberry milk shake. You can also get breakfast items in the morning, like one big huckleberry pancake, egg-filled burritos, and freshly baked cinnamon rolls, but the coffee could peel the chrome off your Harley's tailpipe. If you're in a hurry, this might not be the place for you—the servers and cooks appear to have lead in their pants. Regardless, it's a fun place, and there's live music out on the patio on weekends during the warmer months.

◖ **Wallace Brewing Company** (610 Bank St., Wallace, 208/660-3430, www.wallacebrewing.com, 1–6 P.M. Tues.–Thurs., 1–8 P.M. Fri.–Sat.) is the place to go for locally handcrafted beers. The delicious array includes Jack Leg Stout, Vindicator IPA, and Red Light, a honey wheat lager that pays homage to the town's former ladies of the evening.

Information

The **Historic Wallace Chamber of Commerce** (10 River St., Wallace, 208/753-7151, www.wallaceidahochamber.com) operates a visitors center right off I-90 Exit 61. Next door is the **Mining Heritage Exhibition,** a free park with an array of brightly painted old mining equipment and some picnic tables.

LOOKOUT PASS

Lookout Pass Ski and Recreation Area (208/744-1301, www.skilookout.com, 9 A.M.–4 P.M. daily mid-Dec.–New Year, 9 A.M.–4 P.M. Thurs.–Sun. the rest of the season, closed Christmas Day), at I-90 Exit 0, right on the state line, may be small in stature, but it's big in heart. The state's second-oldest ski area, Lookout has been faithfully serving Silver Valley since 1938. Over much of its life, the area owed its existence to the volunteer efforts of the Idaho Ski Club and others. It is famous for its family-friendly atmosphere and offers skiing, snowmobiling, and other winter activities as well as summer fun like mountain biking. It's the main outfitting point for the Route of the Hiawatha cycling trail.

Alpine Skiing

Although this is a humble mountain in some ways, the snow quality and quantity—a whopping 387 inches per year average—are excellent, and the sweeping views into two states provide a real "high mountain" feeling, despite a peak elevation under 6,000 feet. Lookout Pass recently expanded a bit and now has about 18 runs (the longest is 1.2 miles) and 1,150 feet of vertical drop served by a rope tow and two double chairs. The mountain's back side sports a snowboard and ski terrain park.

Lift tickets (weekend $35 adults, $25 juniors and seniors) won't break your budget, and midweek rates are a few bucks less. Half-day tickets and various special promotional tickets are available too. You can also find ski and snowboard rentals, lessons, and day care services.

The day lodge is cozy and well-kept, offering both food and drink. The bar's lively social scene is especially friendly and intimate, since most of the patrons are locals who know one another. The season here generally runs mid-November–late March or early April.

Cross-Country Skiing

A 16-mile system of cross-country ski trails, ranging in difficulty from beginner to advanced, is accessible from the resort's base area.

Some are shared with snowmobiles. Cross-country skiers can purchase a single-ride lift ticket ($7) and ski their way back down to the base area on the trails.

U.S. 95 to Lake Pend Oreille

HAYDEN LAKE

Heading north on U.S. 95 from Coeur d'Alene, you'll soon come to the turnoff to the town of Hayden Lake, a wealthy bedroom community of Coeur d'Alene. The lakeshore is ringed with expensive homes but not much public lakefront, giving the whole area the appearance of an upper-crust country club.

Recreation

In Hayden Lake, babies are born with silver putters in hand. Golf is as natural as breathing here, and you half expect electric golf carts to replace automobiles on the city streets. The chichi Hayden Lake Country Club is private, but the semichichi, semiprivate **Avondale Golf Course** (10745 Avondale Loop Rd., Hayden Lake, 208/772-5963, year-round, $32–53) has been known to accommodate plebeian passers-through on its 6,525-yard, par-72 course.

Hikers in summer and cross-country skiers in winter enjoy the trails at **English Point** (free), a bit of national forest preserved along the lake's north shore. To get here, turn east off U.S. 95 onto Lancaster Road and drive about 3.5 miles to English Point Road.

Accommodations

On the lake's north side, reached by turning east off U.S. 95 at Lancaster Road (the first major intersection north of Hayden junction), is **Bridle Path Manor** (1155 E. Lancaster Rd., Hayden, 208/762-3126, $90–150), a large Tudor–style house on an expansive horse ranch. Horse fanciers can take trail rides through the woods; others can stay in and play billiards or relax by the fireplace. Rates for the five guest rooms include a full breakfast. Kids are welcome.

One of the biggest old mansions on Hayden Lake is now a gloriously refurbished bed-and-breakfast. The **Clark House** (5250 E. Hayden Lake Rd., Hayden, 208/772-3470 or 800/765-4593, www.clarkhouse.com, $149–179) was built in 1910 as a summer home for millionaire F. Lewis Clark and his wife, Winifred. At the time of its completion, the 15,000-square-foot manse was the most expensive residence in Idaho. After extensive reconstruction, it once again recalls its glory days, although the sprawling estate it reigned over has shrunk over the years from 1,400 acres to 12. Rates at the house include a full gourmet breakfast, all guest rooms have private baths, and you'll enjoy king or queen feather beds, fireplaces, Roman tubs built for two, and great views of the lake. Smoking, pets, and children under 12 are not allowed. The B&B's dining room also has a good reputation; it serves three-course dinners (Tues.–Sat., from $29 pp) to both guests and nonguests by reservation.

Camping

Way around the lake's east side is the U.S. Forest Service's **Mokins Bay Campground** (16 sites, $16) on a six-acre lakeshore plot. Take Forest Road 3090, which circles the lake; it's a long dozen or so miles from town to the campground along either the north or south shores—the northern route is probably the best bet.

ATHOL AND VICINITY
◖ Silverwood Theme Park

Silverwood Theme Park (27843 N. U.S. 95, Athol, 208/683-3400, www.silverwood-themepark.com, Sat.–Sun. early and late in the season, daily in peak season, early

Silverwood Theme Park

May–Oct., $42 adults, $22 ages 3–7 and over age 65), a 700-acre amusement park, is literally a scream—let's see you keep your mouth shut on that upside-down corkscrew roller coaster, or on Tremors, a coaster that plummets into the bowels of the earth, or on the Timber Terror, a 55-mph wooden coaster sure to please even the most obsessed roller-meister. Monster, Roundup, Scrambler, Skydiver, and other "high-intensity" rides will scare the living daylights out of you, and the park recently added Aftershock, a new coaster that drops 177 feet at 65 mph into three upside-down loops. Don't miss the magic show or the ice spectacular. In 2003, Silverwood debuted its new **Boulder Beach** water park, with waterslides, a wave pool, lazy river, and tree house–themed kids area. Admission is included in the Silverwood rates.

Those wanting to make a week or weekend of it will find the park's own 126-site RV park ($36) right across the street. Amenities include full hookups, shaded sites, showers, picnic tables, volleyball courts, horseshoe pits, barbecue grills, a laundry, and a small store with propane. Tenters are welcome, with a maximum of two tents per site ($30). Guests receive discounted admission to the amusement park.

Farragut State Park

During World War II the 4,000-acre Farragut State Park (13550 E. Hwy. 54, Athol, 208/683-2425, day-use $5), on the southern shores of Lake Pend Oreille, had a large U.S. Naval Training Center. The site was supposedly "discovered" by Eleanor Roosevelt on a flight from Washington, D.C., to Seattle. FDR was looking for an inland body of water to train submariners in safety, away from the eyes and ears of the enemies. Eleanor saw Lake Pend Oreille and described it to her husband, who deemed it perfect for the task. Construction of the base began in 1942. By the fall of that year, the base's population of 55,000 military personnel made it the second-largest naval training facility in the country and the largest "city" in Idaho. At war's end the base was decommissioned, and in 1964 Farragut State

Park was established, named after Civil War hero Admiral David Farragut (1801–1870), whose important victories on the Gulf Coast and Mississippi River allowed the Union Army to capture and control the region.

Today, the sprawling park, with its many long loop roads and open areas, still retains a military-base ambience. Four separate campgrounds have a total of 135 sites ($14–40) plus several camping cabins ($50–55) that can sleep up to five; the Whitetail campground ($16–18) is closest to the lake, the park's prime recreational attraction. Sunbathing and splashing are favorite activities, and a concessionaire rents pedal boats, rafts, and beach chairs. A boat-launching area is available for those hauling their own vessels. Those who prefer terra firma fun can explore the park's hiking, biking, and horseback-riding trails, and you can rent horses at the Thimbleberry Group Area, off Highway 54 toward the west end of the park. The northside trails wind through beautiful woods, while the south-side trails skirt the lakeshore. In winter, the park sets and grooms 10 miles of mostly flat cross-country ski trails. Unusual offerings here include a model-airplane flying field and a shooting range often used by black-powder enthusiasts (watch for the occasional cannon shot). To get to the park, take Highway 54 four miles east from U.S. 95 at Athol.

Bayview

The little fishing village of Bayview is an uncrowded hideaway. Docks, boats, and fishing resorts ring the calm waters of Scenic Bay, and the views across the lake are superb. Front and center on the water is friendly **Boileau's Resort** (208/683-2213), where you can walk out the dock to the marina bar and grill for a sandwich, a can of beer, and an earful of fish stories.

Although the Naval Training Center has disappeared, the Navy still makes good use of Lake Pend Oreille for submarine research and development. On the south edge of Bayview is the **Naval Surface Warfare Center, Acoustic Research Detachment,** where the Navy develops stealth technology for submarines. Lake Pend Oreille is the ideal spot for such work for a number of reasons, including its deep, still water; flat bottom contour; isothermal temperature profile; low ambient noise; low echo interference; and large, unobstructed operating areas.

To get to Bayview, continue on Highway 54 from Athol through Farragut State Park. Coming from the north, turn east off U.S. 95 at Careywood.

COCOLALLA, SAGLE, AND VICINITY
Cocolalla Lake

Stretching between the towns of Cocolalla and Westmond, this 800-acre lake attracts anglers all year. They come to round up the usual suspects: rainbow, cutthroat, brown, and brook trout; channel catfish; largemouth bass; crappie; and perch. In winter, you'll see the diehards out on the lake bundled up in their snowsuits, drilling holes through the ice to sink a line. In summer, you can launch a boat onto the lake from a ramp at the northeast end.

Round Lake State Park

This small park (208/263-3489, day-use $5) is two miles down Dufort Road, which turns west off U.S. 95 four miles north of Cocolalla. You'll find 53 wooded campsites ($16) ringing beautiful, 58-acre Round Lake. The shallow lake warms up in summer, making for pleasant swimming. Drop a line for brook and rainbow trout, largemouth bass, sunfish, perch, bullhead, and crappie; ice fishing is popular in winter. Hikers and cross-country skiers enjoy seven miles of trails, groomed in winter, that follow the lakeshore or head off into the forest through lush stands of western red cedar, western hemlock, ponderosa pine, Douglas fir, and western larch. Keep your eyes peeled for some of the park's abundant resident wildlife. Winter also brings out ice skaters and sledders; areas are specifically maintained for both activities.

Sagle and Garfield Bay

Another goofy postal story explains Sagle's name. Back in 1900, the first resident to apply for a post office applied for the name Eagle. That name was already taken, so he changed it to Sagle. The town marks the turnoff to Garfield Bay, a great out-of-the-way spot with a couple of character-laden bar-restaurants, a couple of campgrounds, and a small golf course.

Just as you come into Garfield Bay from Sagle, a road branches left and climbs the hill to the north. A short distance down that road, Forest Road 532 branches off to the right and leads to the **Mineral Point Interpretive Trail** (Trail 82), a short and pleasant nature trail winding through groves of Douglas fir, ponderosa pine, Pacific yew, and western red cedar. Along the way you'll find benches where you can sit and enjoy superb views of the lake. This peaceful spot is perfect for a picnic, and chances are good you'll have it all to yourself. The trail connects with another that leads down to the water at the U.S. Forest Service **Green Bay Campground** (3 sites, free). Pick up an interpretive brochure or get more information at the office of the Forest Service **Sandpoint Ranger District** (1500 U.S. 2, Sandpoint, 208/263-5111).

Bottle Bay

This major bay opening onto the northern arm of Lake Pend Oreille is a favorite stop-off of cruise boats and anglers. **Bottle Bay Resort & Marina** (115 Resort Rd., Sagle, 208/263-5916) has a restaurant and a collection of vacation cabins (from $129). The resort also rents out canoes, kayaks, and paddleboats.

Bottle Bay can be reached via Bottle Bay Road—accessed from Sagle or from just across the long bridge from Sandpoint—or via a cut-off from Garfield Bay Road. Bottle Bay Road leads around the lakeshore, approaching Bottle Bay from the north; Garfield Bay Road winds around Gold Mountain and finds its way up to Bottle Bay from the south.

Sandpoint and Vicinity

Sandpoint and Lake Pend Oreille sneak up on the driver heading north up U.S. 95 thanks to dense woods on either side of the highway. When the road rounds the last bend and the view opens up, it's hard to stifle the oohs and aahs. The huge, brilliant-blue lake is ringed by high mountains, and you have to drive right across the water on a very long bridge to enter Sandpoint. What a grand entrance.

The town perches on the lake's northwest shore, on a "sandy point" first noted by Canadian fur trapper and geographer David Thompson in 1808, the same year that the first nonnative settlement was established. When the railroads and timber companies found their way here, the town took root. It's still a mill town, but a couple of other elements add to the economic and cultural mix.

Back in the 1970s, the town's cheap rents and stunning surroundings were discovered by artists. Then recreation-minded visitors latched on to the area's great skiing, fishing, and other outdoor activities. Today, the logger, artist, and outdoor recreationist are all part of a pleasantly diverse cultural tapestry.

Sandpoint is full of outstanding restaurants and lively nightclubs, and it offers a full calendar of performing-arts events.

SIGHTS
Bonner County Historical Museum

A good place to start your study of Sandpoint is the Bonner County Historical Museum (Lakeview Park, 611 S. Ella Ave., Sandpoint, 208/263-2344, 10 A.M.–4 P.M. Tues.–Sat., reduced hours in winter, $3 adults, $1 ages 6–18, free under age 6). Exhibits explain the region's history, beginning with the indigenous Kootenai peoples and continuing through the days of steamboats and railroads. You also can ask the friendly volunteers about the supposed lake creature, called Pend Oreille Paddler.

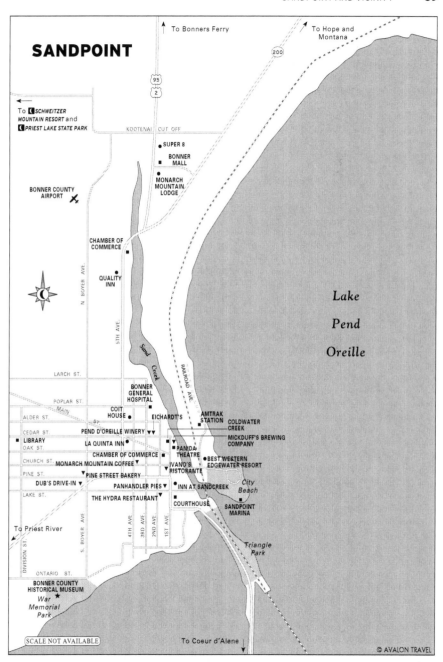

SANDPOINT

To Bonners Ferry

To Hope and Montana

200

95
2

To ◀ SCHWEITZER MOUNTAIN RESORT and ◀ PRIEST LAKE STATE PARK

KOOTENAI CUT OFF

■ SUPER 8

■ BONNER MALL

● MONARCH MOUNTAIN LODGE

BONNER COUNTY AIRPORT ✈

N BOYER AVE.

CHAMBER OF COMMERCE ■

● QUALITY INN

5TH AVE.

Lake

Pend

Oreille

Sand Creek

RAILROAD AVE.

LARCH ST.

BONNER GENERAL HOSPITAL ■

POPLAR ST.

MAIN ST.

COIT HOUSE ●

ALDER ST.

EICHARDT'S ■

AMTRAK STATION ■

COLDWATER CREEK

CEDAR ST.

PEND D'OREILLE WINERY ▼▼

MICKDUFF'S BREWING COMPANY

■ LIBRARY

LA QUINTA INN ●

OAK ST.

CHAMBER OF COMMERCE ■

▼ PANIDA THEATRE

CHURCH ST.

MONARCH MOUNTAIN COFFEE ▼

● BEST WESTERN EDGEWATER RESORT

IVANO'S ▼ RISTORANTE

PINE ST.

▼ PINE STREET BAKERY

City Beach

DUB'S DRIVE-IN ▼

PANHANDLER PIES ▼

● INN AT SANDCREEK

LAKE ST.

THE HYDRA RESTAURANT ■

COURTHOUSE ■

■ SANDPOINT MARINA

4TH AVE.

3RD AVE.

2ND AVE.

1ST AVE.

S BOYER AVE.

To Priest River

Triangle Park

DIVISION ST.

ONTARIO ST.

BONNER COUNTY HISTORICAL MUSEUM

War ★ Memorial Park

To Coeur d'Alene

SCALE NOT AVAILABLE

© AVALON TRAVEL

LAKE PEND OREILLE RECREATION

Largest of the state's lakes, Pend Oreille is 43 miles long and more than 1,100 feet deep in places. In summer, swimmers splash along the shores, sailors glide silently across the clear waters, water-skiers skim over the surface, and anglers troll the depths searching for some of the 14 species of resident game fish.

City Beach

As soon as the hot summer sun arrives, it seems the whole town heads for City Beach. On a July weekend you'll find blankets covering nearly every square inch of this relatively small spit of sand extending out into Lake Pend Oreille. Besides the beach itself, the recreation area includes a playground; areas for basketball, volleyball, and picnicking; and docks from where the lake cruise ships depart. In winter, City Beach takes on a quieter, more contemplative air, but it's still a great place to watch the white-caps on the water and let the chill wind cleanse your spirit. The beach is at the foot of Bridge Street, off U.S. 95 downtown.

Boat Rentals

Sandpoint Marina (120 E. Lake St., Sandpoint, 208/263-1535) at Dover Bay rents ski boats and pontoon boats ($350–650 per day). Hourly rentals with a two-hour minimum are available too. The marina also rents kayaks, canoes, and water-ski equipment.

Scenic Boat Cruises

To get a duck's-eye view of Sandpoint, hook up with **Lake Pend Oreille Cruises** (208/255-5253, www.lakependoreillecruises.com) for 1.5-hour sightseeing cruises (2:30 P.M. daily mid-June–mid-Sept., $19 adults, $18 seniors, and $14 under age 12) aboard the custom-designed *Shawnodese* from the dock at City Beach. Also offered are dinner cruises, eagle-watching cruises, and other seasonal trips; call for a full schedule.

Fishing

Kamloops, kokanee, whitefish, perch, crappie, bluegill, largemouth bass, rainbow, brown, brook trout—whatever your piscatory pleasure, it's waiting for you here. World-record rainbows

Lake Pend Oreille

© IDAHO DIVISION OF TOURISM

and bull trout have been pulled from the lake's depths. You can rent a boat and head out on your own, but it probably makes more sense to avail yourself of local expertise. Fishing guides in the area include **Pend Oreille Charters** (208/265-6781, www.pocharters.com) and **Diamond Charters** (208/265-2565, www.diamondcharters.com).

Kayak Tours

Lake Pend Oreille's many bays and islands make for prime exploring by kayak. **Full Spectrum Tours** (208/263-5975, www.kayaking.net) can teach you kayaking or take you on a tour. Rates range from about $70 for a half-day trip with no food to $450 for a three-day, two-night adventure. The season runs June–September. They also rent kayaks and canoes ($25–40 for 2 hours).

OTHER RECREATION
Golf

The Lower Pack River meanders through the golf links at **The Idaho Club** (151 Clubhouse Way, Sandpoint, 208/265-8600 or 800/323-7020, $80–145), creating periodic water hazards on 15 of the course's 18 holes. This semiprivate golf resort gives first dibs to its members, who have vacation homes on the property, but the 6,923-yard, par-71 course is open to the public. Greens fees for nonmembers vary by season and include a cart. Your tee shots might be critiqued by some of the area's abundant wildlife, including elk, deer, bald eagles, and ospreys. The moose play through. Traversing the fairways of the scenic course, you'll play past stands of cedar and birch, the latter glimmering gold in fall. To get to The Idaho Club, take Highway 200 east from Sandpoint about seven miles and turn left just past milepost 37.

For a quick nine holes, head to **Elks Golf Course** (30196 Hwy. 200 E., Sandpoint, 208/263-4321, around $16). The par-35 course plays a little under 3,000 yards.

Hiking and Biking

One of the best places for a hike, run, or bike ride in town is also one of the easiest to get to. The **Long Bridge** that you drove into town

City Beach in Sandpoint

© IDAHO DIVISION OF TOURISM

on has a pedestrian and bike path along the east side of it. To access the trail from downtown, follow signs from the foot of Lake Street. **Outdoor Experience** (314 N. 1st Ave., Sandpoint, 208/263-6028) rents cruiser bikes ($35 per day, $20 for 2 hours).

Sandpoint Ranger District (1500 U.S. 2, Sandpoint, 208/263-5111) has pamphlets about the area's hiking and mountain biking trails, some of which are described in this guide.

South of town across the lake, the 3.7-mile one-way **Gold Hill Trail** (Trail 3) climbs the northern flanks of Gold Hill, providing panoramic views of the city and the lake. The lower trailhead is on Bottle Bay Road, about five miles north of Sagle. To get to the upper trailhead, take Sagle Road six miles to Contest Mountain Road (Forest Rd. 2642) and follow that road six more miles to the trailhead.

North of town, the easy 0.5-mile one-way **Caribou Lake Trail** (Trail 58) leads to a small lake in the Selkirks north of Schweitzer Mountain Resort. Take U.S. 95 north from town 13 miles to Pack River Road. Follow that road five miles to Caribou Creek Road (Forest Rd. 2684), and continue down that rough road seven miles to the trailhead.

East of town, the long **Round Top-Bee Top Trail** (Trail 120) is especially popular among mountain bikers. The route traverses a long, high divide linking Trestle Peak, Round Top, Cougar Peak, and Bee Top. It's about 20 miles long and provides many great views from its 6,000-foot heights. The northwest trailhead is on Forest Road 275, which leaves Highway 200 at Trestle Creek between Sandpoint and Hope. Look for the trailhead at a hairpin turn in the road about 15 miles in. The southeast trailhead is off Lightning Creek Road (Forest Rd. 419), about five miles north from Clark Fork.

Outfitters

For backcountry gear, head to **Outdoor Experience** (314 N. 1st Ave., Sandpoint, 208/263-6028). The full-line adventure-gear store sells packs, mountain bikes, and backcountry duds, and also rents cross-country skis,

snowshoes, telemark skis, and kayaks. Bike mechanics are on duty here seven days a week. **Sports Plus** (819 U.S. 2, Sandpoint, 208/263-5174) is a local favorite selling water-skis, skateboards, and mountain bikes. Bike mechanics are on duty. Schweitzer Mountain Resort (10000 Schweitzer Mountain Rd., Sandpoint, 208/255-3081) is the best place to rent alpine skis and snowboards.

ENTERTAINMENT AND EVENTS
Entertainment

The **Panida Theatre** (300 N. 1st Ave., Sandpoint, 208/263-9191, www.panida.org) is the focus of Sandpoint's flourishing entertainment scene. The beautiful Spanish Mission–style theater hosted vaudeville and movies after its construction in 1927. Age took its toll over the years, but in 1985 the city purchased the theater and is in the process of restoring it to its former glory. Today, the Panida is on the National Register of Historic Places and stages local drama productions, a foreign- and art-film series, concerts by touring and local musicians, and many other special events. The theater's name is a combination of *pan* from Panhandle and *ida* from Idaho, but nevertheless it's pronounced "PAN-idda."

Eichardt's (212 Cedar St., Sandpoint, 208/263-4005, nightly) is the most reliable place to hear live music, especially if you like blues.

Events

In early August, the big 10-day **Festival at Sandpoint** (208/265-4554 or 888/265-4554, www.festivalatsandpoint.com) concert series takes place at Memorial Field. The 2010 lineup included Brandi Carlile, Big Bad Voodoo Daddy, and Michael Franti and Spearhead. The **Pend Oreille Arts and Crafts Fair** brightens City Beach the first weekend in August with a bevy of locally produced paintings, photography, jewelry, and pottery.

On the cold side of the calendar, Sandpoint's five-day **Winter Carnival** celebrates snow season with snow sculptures, snowshoe softball, and a torchlight parade. It all takes place at the tail end of January.

For a complete calendar of events, contact the **Greater Sandpoint Chamber of Commerce** (208/263-2161 or 800/800-2106, www.sandpointchamber.org).

SHOPPING

Wolf sweatshirts, moose clocks, Native American jewelry, and much, much more—**Coldwater Creek** (311 N. 1st Ave., Sandpoint, 208/263-2265, www.coldwatercreek.com) carries nature-inspired goods of every description, but it's probably best known for its line of women's apparel and fashion accessories. One of Sandpoint's biggest employers, this mail-order and national mall retailer has its flagship store in a two-story brick building downtown. There's even a wine bar, where you can unwind after a frenzied shopping spree.

Zany Zebra (317 N. Main St., Sandpoint, 208/263-2178) sells tie-dye, hemp Hacky Sacks, funky art postcards, cool clothing, and more.

Named after one of the great Northwest trappers, **Finan McDonald Clothing Company** (301 N. 1st Ave., Sandpoint, 208/263-3622) is an upscale store carrying stylish outdoor clothing and accessories for men and women.

The Corner Book Store (106 Main St., Sandpoint, 208/265-2886) sells new and used books of all genres. This is a great place to hang out and peruse the shelves for those hard-to-find titles.

Art Galleries

Sandpoint enjoys a reputation as an art colony, and some 15 galleries are scattered through the downtown area. A couple of favorites are **First Light Gallerie** (302 N. 1st Ave., Sandpoint, 208/263-7148), which spotlights the remarkable acrylic and watercolor paintings of Scott Kirby and photography by Do Verdier, and **Art Works** (214 N. 1st Ave., Sandpoint, 208/263-2642), a local artists' co-op gallery offering an eclectic collection of paintings, sculpture, pottery, jewelry, wood and glass works, and more.

Many local galleries, restaurants, and shops participate in **Artwalk** (208/263-6139, www.artinsandpoint.org) a self-guided art tour of the town. You can pick up a list of the featured artists, their respective media, and the locations of their works at the chamber of commerce or many of the galleries around town.

ACCOMMODATIONS

Summer is peak season in Sandpoint, and summer rates are listed; winter rates are significantly lower.

$50-100

Quality Inn (807 N. 5th Ave., Sandpoint, 208/263-2111 or 800/635-2534, from $69 d) is in a hectic location right on U.S. 2/95. It's got an indoor pool, a decent restaurant, and 62 guest rooms. **Super 8 Motel** (476841 U.S. 95 N., Sandpoint, 208/263-2210, $49–99) has 60 guest rooms and a hot tub. Children 12 and under stay free when accompanied by an adult.

In the Bonner Mall area on the way to Schweitzer, you'll find **Monarch Mountain Lodge** (363 Bonner Mall Way, Sandpoint, 208/263-1222 or 866/756-1222, www.monarchmountainsandpoint.com, $69–105), offering 48 guest rooms, two spas, a sauna, and a free continental breakfast. Some guest rooms have fireplaces.

$100-150

The 1907 **◖ Coit House** (502 N. 4th Ave., Sandpoint, 208/265-4035, www.coithouse.com, $89–150) is a B&B within easy walking distance of downtown. The creaky, character-filled Victorian is full of antiques, and each guest room has its own bath, cable TV, and phone. Rates include a full breakfast featuring fresh-baked breads. Children under 12 are discouraged, and discounts are offered for longer stays. Smoking is allowed outside only.

The **◖ Inn at Sand Creek** (105 S. 1st Ave., Sandpoint, 208/255-2821, www.innatsandcreek.com, from $99) offers three guest rooms, two with Victorian decor and one with Western decor, and a condo. Two of the guest rooms have a fireplace, and all have cable TV. Amenities include a hot tub, a sun deck, and a picnic-barbecue area. Smoking is not allowed.

Best Western Edgewater Resort (56 Bridge St., Sandpoint, 208/263-3194 or 800/635-2534, from $107 d) enjoys a prime piece of lakefront real estate overlooking City Beach, just a block from downtown. All 54 guest rooms face the water and offer either a private balcony or a private patio; for a luxurious splurge, try one of the suites with a jetted tub or a fireplace. The resort has an indoor pool, and rates include continental breakfast. The inn's Trinity restaurant is a great place for dinner or a sunset cocktail.

$150-250
La Quinta Inn (415 Cedar St., Sandpoint, 208/263-9581 or 800/282-0660, from $189 d) is right in the heart of downtown. Amenities include a heated pool, a whirlpool tub, and an adjacent restaurant open for breakfast, lunch, and dinner daily.

Western Pleasure Guest Ranch (1413 Upper Gold Creek Rd., Sandpoint, 208/263-9066, www.westernpleasureranch.com, call for rates) sits on a 960-acre spread about 16 miles northeast of town. The working cattle ranch has been around since 1940. Summer trail rides through forest inhabited by deer, elk, bears, moose, and wild turkeys lead to views of Lake Pend Oreille and the Selkirks. Winter sleigh rides are provided courtesy of a beautiful team of Percherons; the horses pull guests through whitewashed woods on a 45-minute ride culminating in hot drinks and popcorn. Cross-country ski trails are also set up and groomed in winter.

Accommodations are in either modern log cabins or a new lodge building. Each of the cabins has a full kitchen and woodstove and can accommodate up to six people. The 10,000-square-foot lodge sports a massive river-rock fireplace and has six guest rooms. In summer season, late June–mid-September, package stays are offered that include daily rides, evening entertainment, lodging, and all meals with a three-night minimum. Packages

without the trail rides and packages with breakfast only are also available.

Vacation Rentals
North Idaho Property Solutions (877/223-0345, www.nivacationrentals.com) lists rentals of float homes, cottages, and condos in a variety of price ranges.

CAMPING AND RVING
On the south side of the long bridge, Lakeshore Drive leads west around Murphy Bay to the Corps of Engineers' **Springy Point Recreation Area** and its campground (reservations 877/444-6777, 38 sites, mid-May–Labor Day, $18, no hookups).

FOOD AND DRINK
Upscale Fare
Walk into **The Hydra Steakhouse** (115 Lake St., Sandpoint, 208/263-7123, lunch Tues.–Fri., dinner daily, entrées $12–32) and you'll think you're in a plant-filled grotto. The rambling interior is done up in green with lots of wood, and subdued lighting adds to the aura of cool tranquility. The menu offers steak, chicken, seafood, and pasta entrées plus a large salad bar. A good wine list offers several selections by the glass, and a half-dozen microbrews are on tap in the lounge.

Trinity at City Beach (58 Bridge St., Sandpoint, 208/255-7558, www.trinityatcity-beach.com, breakfast, lunch, and dinner daily, dinner entrées $15–26), in the Best Western Edgewater Resort, has a stylish dining room with killer views of the lake. During the day, the menu focuses on breakfast and typical lunch fare. At night, the restaurant gets serious with high-end entrées like langostino ravioli, hazelnut-crusted trout, and prime rib with Parmesan mashed potatoes. The wine list boasts lots of European and Northwestern labels.

 The Bistro/Inn at Sand Creek (105 S. 1st Ave., Sandpoint, 208/265-2277, 4–9:30 P.M. Wed., 1–9:30 P.M. Thurs.–Sat., brunch 10 A.M.–3:30 P.M. Sun., entrées $17–30) puts out contemporary Northwestern fare. The menu emphasizes locally grown produce and other regional foodstuffs. In summer you might find dishes like wild salmon tartar, pan-seared chicken breast with cornbread panzanella, and an Idaho Wagyu (Kobe) New York steak crowned with blue cheese butter.

Casual Dining

It's hard to beat **Eichardt's** (212 Cedar St., Sandpoint, 208/263-4005, from 11:30 A.M. daily, under $15), a pub and grill suitable for all but the fanciest night out. The restaurant pours a dozen great microbrews, including pale ales, IPAs, ESBs, and thick cream stouts. The wide-ranging menu includes burgers, sandwiches, steaks, and seafood. The atmosphere is warm and casual, and Eichardt's regularly hosts live music on weekend nights.

MickDuff's Brewing Company (312 N. 1st Ave., Sandpoint, 208/255-4351, www.mickduffs.com, lunch and dinner daily, $7–15) is a great spot for a burger and a handcrafted beer. This downtown brewpub serves lots of burgers, hot sandwiches, finger food, steaks, and grilled salmon with onion rings. The brewmasters here make a rotating selection of ales, porters, and stouts.

Wine Bars

One of the best boutique wineries in Idaho happens to be in Sandpoint. **(Pend d'Oreille Winery** (220 Cedar St., Sandpoint, 208/265-8545, www.powine.com, 10 A.M.–6:30 P.M. Mon.–Thurs., 10 A.M.–8 P.M. Fri.–Sat., 11 A.M.–6 P.M. Sun.) has a comfy tasting room and wine bar downtown. You can sample the offerings of winemaker Steve Meyer, who produces an array of varietal red and white wines, blends, and a few sweet wines, like an extremely drinkable Huckleberry Blush. Most of his wines are made from Columbia Valley grapes. The place even serves a light menu of wine-friendly food.

As promised, there's a small wine bar at Coldwater Creek (311 N. 1st Ave., Sandpoint, 208/255-1293) that pours a wide variety of wines by the glass, including many vintages from the Northwest. You also can get appetizers and panini sandwiches.

Ethnic Cuisine

Ivano's Ristorante (102 S. 1st Ave., Sandpoint, 208/263-0211, lunch Mon.–Fri., dinner daily, $12–26) is an excellent Italian joint with an elegant but comfortable atmosphere. The upscale menu offers appetizers, various pasta dishes, and entrées of chicken, veal, seafood, and steak.

Jalapeño's (314 N. 2nd Ave., Sandpoint, 208/263-2995, lunch and dinner daily, dinner entrées $8–12) is the local favorite for Mexican food. It's geared toward the Yanqui palate, perhaps, but offers large portions and reasonable prices.

Get your Thai fix at **Bangkok Cuisine** (202 N. 2nd Ave., Sandpoint, 208/265-4149, lunch Mon.–Fri., dinner Mon.–Sat., dinner entrées $8–14), where you can find MSG-free dishes with or without meat, either spicy or mild. Beer and wine are available.

Pizza

Second Avenue Pizza (215 S. 2nd Ave., Sandpoint, 208/263-9321, lunch and dinner daily) serves decent pizza pies and cold beer. Here you can get creative veggie concoctions like the Schweitzer Mountain Ski Flakes Special, which includes "fresh spinach, tomatoes avalanched with feta cheese, garlic, moguls of mushrooms, black olives, and at the peak—knee deep in asiago cheese." Seven or so microbrews on tap help wash it down in style. The restaurant is nonsmoking.

Burgers and Sandwiches

Dub's Drive-In (U.S. 2 W. and Boyer St., Sandpoint, 208/263-4300, daily) is a Sandpoint institution offering traditional artery-clogging burgers in sizes suitable for big and little tykes alike. For dessert or a summer cooler, try a soft ice-cream cone.

You can also clog your arteries downtown at **(Joe's Authentic Philly Cheesesteaks** (102 Church St., Sandpoint, 208/263-1444, 10 A.M.–8 P.M. daily, under $10). This little shop puts out several variations of the City of Brotherly Love's most famous sandwich, as well as hoagies, burgers, and Reubens.

MCMANUS MUSES ABOUT THE SELKIRK MOUNTAINS

Outdoor humorist Patrick McManus, who hails from Sandpoint in Idaho's Panhandle, has made a living out of adding levity and wit to potentially fatal situations associated with outdoor fun. He has written 13 books about the lighter side of the great outdoors, including *Never Sniff A Gift Fish*, *How I Got This Way*, and *They Shoot Canoes, Don't They?* Besides penning nonfiction books (he admits to some fictional embellishment), McManus has also been an editor at *Field & Stream* magazine and a longtime columnist for *Outdoor Life* magazine, in which he wrote the hilarious kicker "The Last Laugh." In recent years, he has tried his hand at writing mystery novels and even a children's book. McManus, who now lives in nearby Spokane, Washington, offers this humorous recollection about the mountains near his hometown:

When I was a boy camping in the Selkirk Mountains, the range contained at least one grizzly bear. I know this because our rural postman was once treed by it. He was a large and flabby man, so it was hard for me to imagine him scurrying up a tree, but he explained that the sight of a grizzly headed your way can virtually flood you with such energy and enthusiasm for climbing that you could zip up a dozen such trees, if any of them proved unsatisfactory. I explored the Selkirks from the time I was 12 until I went off to college and can report there was not a single dark night our postman's grizzly did not populate my thoughts.

Breakfast and Coffee

The best bet for a full breakfast is **Panhandler Pies** (120 S. 1st Ave., Sandpoint, 208/263-2912, 6:30 A.M.–10 P.M. Mon.–Sat., under $10), which offers a full menu for breakfast, lunch, and dinner and bakes 23 different kinds of pie for dessert.

On the edge of downtown, one step removed from the beaten path, is **Monarch Mountain Coffee** (208 N. 4th Ave., Sandpoint, 208/265-9382, daily). It's a spacious, bright, and shiny place great for writing that postcard to the folks back home. Plus the coffeehouse roasts its own beans and serves freshly baked goods and light breakfast items.

Speaking of yummy baked treats, **Pine Street Bakery** (710 Pine St., Sandpoint, 208/263-9012) keeps its ovens full with fresh croissants, sweet pastries, cookies, tarts, and loaves of rustic bread. The bakery also serves espresso drinks and Tazzina teas.

Groceries

The **Farmers Market at Sandpoint** (9 A.M.–1 P.M. Sat. and 3–5:30 P.M. Wed.

May–Oct.) fills Farmin Park (3rd Ave. and Oak St., Sandpoint) with fresh produce, eggs, prepared foodstuffs, fresh-cut flowers, and crafts.

Foodies definitely need to check out **Pend Oreille Pasta & Wine** (476534 U.S. 95, Sandpoint, 208/263-1352, www.pendoreillepasta.com, 9 A.M.–6 P.M. Mon.–Sat.). This specialty food store and wine shop carries sausages, artisanal cheeses, freshly baked breads, cured olives, and prepared pasta dinners. Finding that perfect bottle of vino is not a problem here.

For natural foods, bulk foods, vitamins, juices, and organic health products, try **Winter Ridge Natural Foods** (703 W. Lake St., Sandpoint, 208/265-8135).

INFORMATION

The **Greater Sandpoint Chamber of Commerce** (231 N. 3rd Ave., Sandpoint, 208/263-2161 or 800/800-2106, www.sandpointchamber.org) keeps a small visitors center across from Farmin Park. Recreation information is available from the U.S. Forest Service

Sandpoint Ranger District (1500 U.S. 2, Sandpoint, 208/263-5111). Sandpoint's gorgeous **public library** (1407 Cedar St., Sandpoint, 208/263-6930) offers free Internet access and a relaxing space to peruse periodicals (a ski magazine, perhaps?).

GETTING THERE

To reach the **Amtrak** station (450 Railroad Ave., Sandpoint, 800/872-7245), turn left off Bridge Street, which is just across Sand Creek on your way toward City Beach. Amtrak's *Empire Builder* stops on its run from Chicago to Seattle or Portland. Eastbound trains arrive at 2:32 A.M. daily, westbound trains arrive at 11:49 P.M. daily. The closest lodging to the train station—within bleary-eyed, suitcase-lugging stumbling distance—is the Best Western Edgewater Resort.

◖ SCHWEITZER MOUNTAIN RESORT

High in the Selkirk Mountains, a short 11-mile drive north of town, is Schweitzer Mountain Resort (10000 Schweitzer Mountain Rd., Sandpoint, 208/263-9555, snow report 208/265-9562, www.schweitzer.com). One of Idaho's top ski areas, Schweitzer offers a vertical drop of 2,400 feet, two massive bowls, and outstanding base-area lodging and dining. After the snow melts, you can come up the hill for hiking, horseback riding, and even lift-served mountain biking.

Alpine Skiing and Snowboarding

Seemingly underused, Schweitzer's lifts seldom have any appreciable lines. The resort's new high-speed "six-pack" chair (the first in Idaho, nicknamed "Stella") plus a single detachable quad, four double chairs, and two handle tows serve 2,500 acres of terrain and 59 named runs rated at 20 percent beginner, 40 percent intermediate, 35 percent advanced, and 5 percent expert. More than half the runs are groomed, including some of the steep upper slopes, by means of winch cats. The longest run measures a quad-burning 2.7 miles. Racing enthusiasts can try out the NASTAR

© IDAHO DIVISION OF TOURISM

Schweitzer Mountain Resort, playing host to a music festival

course, while snowboarders enjoy the resort's terrain park.

Full-day lift tickets cost around $65 adults, $55 seniors and college students with ID, $49 ages 7–17, free under age 7. Two lifts are lighted for night skiing Friday–Saturday and holiday evenings until 9 P.M. Lessons and a wide range of rental equipment such as skis, snowboards, tele-gear, and snowshoes are available at the base area. The resort offers day-care services (208/255-3038) and discounted beginner packages including rentals, lessons, and lift tickets.

Cross-Country Skiing

Schweitzer sets and grooms 19 miles of cross-country trails just to the north of the base area. The trails are better groomed than any Park N' Ski area and offer great views and pleasant, rolling terrain. The well-marked trails leave the busy lodge area and climb around the ridge to the north. Both a wide skating lane and traditional tracks are set up. An all-day trail pass costs $12 adults, $10 seniors and ages 7–17; rental gear is available.

Mountain Biking

Schweitzer maintains 20 miles of mountain-bike trails on the resort property, and those trails connect with many more miles of logging roads that wind through the Selkirks. You can rent top-notch bikes at Schweitzer for about $50 per half day, $85 per full day. Those who love the downhill but loathe the uphill can load their fat-tire friend onto the resort's quad chair-lift and get a ride to the top ($20 for an all-day pass). For more information, call the activity center at 208/255-3081.

Horseback Riding

Mountain Horse Adventures (208/263-8768, www.mountainhorseadventures.com) offers guided horse treks around the mountains here in summer. Three-hour rides cost $60.

Hiking

In summer, the hills around Schweitzer are bursting with berries and wildflowers. Add panoramic views of Lake Pend Oreille and you've got ideal hiking country. Ten miles of trails meander through the hills. Those who want the mountaintop views without the toil can ride the resort's quad chair to the summit for around $10, then enjoy a downhill stroll.

Free trail maps are available at the base area, and guided hikes are sometimes offered on Saturday mornings in July–August.

Accommodations

Schweitzer Mountain Bed & Breakfast (110 Crystal Court, Sandpoint, 208/263-7117, $110–280) is up Crystal Springs Road from the main Schweitzer parking lot. This mountaintop B&B has five guest rooms, each with a private bath. Amenities include a hot tub, a TV room, and ski-in, ski-out access. Rates include breakfast, as well as tea, coffee, and beverages throughout the day. Smoking, children, and pets are not allowed.

The resort has two slope-side lodges and condos in the base area. The **Selkirk Lodge** (10000 Schweitzer Mountain Rd., Sandpoint, 877/487-4643, $210–293 peak season) sits right at the base of the lifts, its tall gabled roof giving it the air of a Bavarian château. Some guest rooms have jetted tubs, and there's an outdoor heated pool and hot tub complex. The newer **White Pine Lodge** (10000 Schweitzer Mountain Rd., Sandpoint, 877/487-4643, $330–578 peak season) has 1–3-bedroom accommodations, plus outdoor hot tubs and a shopping and dining village.

Highway 200: Pend Oreille Scenic Byway

HOPE AND VICINITY

East of Sandpoint, Highway 200 skirts the north shore of Lake Pend Oreille, soon coming to Hope, East Hope, and even Beyond Hope. On a warm summer's day, this area of big trees and big water is sublime. Perhaps that's why famed Canadian geographer and explorer David Thompson built the very first fur-trading outpost in Idaho, Kullyspell House, on the Hope peninsula way back in 1809. Today, Thompson is commemorated here with the David Thompson Game Preserve. Also on the peninsula are posh homes hidden away in the woods, a superb national forest campground, and great views of the lake at every turn.

Accommodations

C Red Fir Resort (1147 Red Fir Rd., Hope, 208/264-5287, www.redfirresort.com, Apr.–Nov., $95–165) is a little gem tucked away on the secluded northwest side of the Hope Peninsula, facing Ellisport Bay and the Cabinet Mountains beyond. Twelve cabins perch on a quiet and gentle tree-covered slope overlooking the lake. The cabins vary in size, with some sleeping up to eight; a few are below and above this range. Each cabin has a private deck, a barbecue, a full kitchen, and a bath. The resort also has its own dock and swimming area.

Right next to the Floating Restaurant, **Pend**

Oreille Shores Resort (47390 Hwy. 200, Hope, 208/264-5828, www.posresort.com, $155–230) is a plush condo development on the lake. Each of the 51 units has a kitchen, a washer and dryer, a stereo, cable TV, and a fireplace. An on-site athletic club features an indoor pool, hot tubs, racquetball and tennis courts, a sauna, and a weight room.

Camping and RVing

Out on the Hope peninsula, you'll find an RV park and a superbly located National Forest campground. To get to the peninsula, continue east two miles past Hope and watch for the Sam Owen Road turnoff on the right. Especially appealing here is the area's status as a game refuge. In the early morning and evening hours, large numbers of nearly tame deer feed on the grassy hills, very near to the Winnebagos and awestruck, clucking campers. Keep your camera ready.

Island View RV Resort (1767 Peninsula Rd., Hope, 208/264-5509, year-round) has 60 sites ($35–40) with full hookups. The resort also has a marina, gas, boat rentals, a rec room, a small store, a laundry, and hot showers.

Also on the Hope peninsula, the Forest Service's **Sam Owen Campground** ($16–20) offers million-dollar lakefront property. This is without a doubt the Ritz of the state's Forest Service campgrounds. Locals love it, so it fills up in summer, but it's a big area and the sites are large. Head straight for the Skipping Stone Loop; units 32, 33, and 35 are among the choicest, just steps from the water. The area also makes a great day-use ($5) destination. For more information call the USFS **Sandpoint Ranger District** (208-263-5111, reservations 877/444-6777 or www.recreation.gov).

Houseboat Rentals

You could spend a far worse one-week vacation than lazily cruising Lake Pend Oreille with some friends on a houseboat. **North Idaho Boat & Home Vacations** (1245 Hwy. 200, Hope, 208/755-0970, www.sandpointhouse-boats.com), at Hope Marine Services, rents small (15-foot, sleeps 8) and large (32-foot,

sleeps 10) houseboats. In peak summer season, houseboats cost around $400 per day; multi-day packages are available, which brings the price down slightly. A refundable $500 damage deposit is required. All boats have a propane barbecue, a swim ladder and water slide, an AM/FM radio and CD player, a VHF radio, charts, a fishfinder, and all safety equipment. The layout includes a full kitchen, a bathroom, a stateroom, a living room, and a full-length sundeck up top. You may never want to come home. The company also has rental properties on terra firma.

Food

Known all over the Panhandle as "the Floater," the ◖ **Floating Restaurant** (Hwy. 200, East Hope, 208/264-5311, lunch and dinner daily, brunch Sun. Apr.–Oct., dinner entrées $15–22), at Hope Marine Services, is a local landmark. You walk out on a creaky-tippy dock to it, past sailboats and motorboats and rowboats, and then sit either inside or out on the big marina-side deck. The seafood seems appropriate—try the scrumptious Copper River salmon with orange-ginger sauce or a Caesar salad with grilled prawns. The food is good, but ah, the atmosphere. Kick back with a good microbrew or glass of wine; watch the sun set over the boats bobbing in the harbor; listen to the cry of the seagulls so far from Pacific shores.

CLARK FORK AND VICINITY

Clark Fork is the last outpost of civilization you'll pass through before crossing into Montana. The town enjoys a scenic location in the shadow of the Cabinet Mountains, at the confluence of the Clark Fork River and picturesque Lightning Creek. "Downtown" has a couple of stores and taverns but not much else. A couple of RV parks are in the vicinity.

Cabinet Gorge Dam

Virtually at the Idaho-Montana border, this is the last point of interest along Highway 200 before you leave the state behind and venture into Montana. The dam is 208 feet high and 600 feet long and backs up the 20-mile-long Clark

Fork Reservoir, almost entirely in Montana. The spectacle of the water surging through narrow Cabinet Gorge is powerful indeed. Imagine what it must have looked like when ancient glacial Lake Missoula broke through to carve out the gorge in the first place.

Hiking

A popular and strenuous trail starts outside Clark Fork and leads to the top of **Scotchman Peak,** a 7,000-foot sentry watching over Lake Pend Oreille to the west and the lofty Montana skyline to the east. The views from the summit can't be beat. The trail is only seven miles round-trip but climbs some 3,700 vertical feet in less than four miles. To reach the trailhead, follow Clark Fork's Main Street north. It soon turns into Forest Road 276. Continue past the turnoff to the University of Idaho's Forestry Field Campus. When the road forks about a mile farther down the road, bear right, following signs to Trail 65. One mile farther, turn left on Forest Road 2294A, then turn left again 0.5 miles down that road. After a little over two miles, make one last left and proceed 220 yards to the trailhead. If all that seems too confusing, ask the rangers at the Sandpoint Ranger District Office in Sandpoint to draw you a map.

Huckleberry Tent and Breakfast

You read it right: This business (180 Thunderbolt Dr., Clark Fork, 208/266-0155, www.huckleberrytentandbreakfast.com, Apr. 15–Nov. 15) specializes in tents and breakfast among the huckleberry bushes. Stay the night in a decked-out canvas tent ($125 d) with nearby fire rings, wonderful mountain views, and no TVs or other modern devices to distract you from the great outdoors. Wake up to a big homespun breakfast, which will probably include huckleberries in late summer.

U.S. 2 WEST

West of Sandpoint, U.S. 2 follows the lazy and scenic Pend Oreille River down to the town of Priest River and on to the Washington state line. In the town of **Laclede,** named after a French engineer on the Great Northern Railway, is the Corps of Engineers–built **Riley Creek Recreation Area,** where you'll find a campground (reservations 877/444-6777, 67 sites, mid-May–Labor Day, $24 with hookups). Laclede is also well known to **rock climbing** enthusiasts for Laclede Rocks, right off the highway two miles west of Laclede. The area has a couple of easy routes, but most are in the 5.8–5.10 range. One 5.12 top-rope problem challenges the very skilled. Come in summer when it's hot and you can end your climb by jumping into the nearby Pend Oreille River.

Like Priest Lake, the town of **Priest River** was named in honor of Jesuit priest and early area missionary Father John Roothaan. Logging has long been its lifeblood; great log drives down the Priest River once fed the big mills here. Today the town is in the process of sprucing itself up for a tourist economy.

West of Priest River is **Albeni Falls Dam,** another Corps of Engineers project built in 1951. As the dam was built right at the falls, the falls themselves are now gone. In summer, free tours of the dam are offered daily at the powerhouse (208/437-3133).

Priest Lake

Surrounded by the dense forests and lofty, snowcapped peaks of the Selkirks, Priest Lake is a secluded, off-the-beaten-path gem. There are no cities along the lakeshore, and the biggest towns on the lake, Coolin and Nordman, are not much more than small supply stations for anglers, campers, and the few hardy souls who live up here.

The area is a haven for wildlife. Black bears are common at the lake, and a few grizzlies roam the high country around the periphery. Deer and moose are plentiful, mountain goats inhabit rocky crags near the east shore, and a small herd of endangered woodland caribou survives tenuously in the wildest reaches of this northern realm; wildlife photographers will love it.

The lake is also a favorite of anglers, who fish for lunker mackinaw in forest-shaded coves along the lake's edge. Campers looking for solitude camp on one of several islands in the lake, or they boat or hike north to Upper Priest Lake. The upper lake—connected to the much larger lower lake by a two-mile-long narrow and shallow channel called the Thorofare—is preserved for the wilderness experience. Waterskiing and jet skiing are prohibited on the upper lake, where canoes are the vessels of choice. Trails through cool, dense forest lead between the lower and upper lakes to campgrounds reached only by boat or on foot.

Around the shore of the lower lake you'll find numerous resorts, lodgings, and campgrounds of varying degrees of luxury as well as several marinas and a couple of villages offering convivial contact with members of your own species. Many of the restaurants feature huckleberry dishes of every description. Priest Lake is huckleberry heaven—people come from all over the region in mid–late summer to pick the delectable fruit.

◖ PRIEST LAKE STATE PARK

Historical sites, natural-history interpretive information, and abundant recreation opportunities make Priest Lake State Park (day-use

Priest Lake

$5) an outstanding destination. Two of the three units of the park are found along the lake's east shore.

Park headquarters is at the **Indian Creek Unit,** 11 miles north of Coolin on East Shore Road. Once a logging camp for the Diamond Match Company, the site displays a remnant of the logging operation—a section of the old flume, built in 1946, that once floated logs into the lake from up to three miles away.

The campground's broad sandy beach attracts swimmers and sunbathers; others prefer to hike one of the two easy hiking trails meandering through the woods or play volleyball or basketball on the campground's courts. A boat-launching ramp lets you float your boat. Throughout summer, the interpretive center presents a full slate of events, including educational campfire programs, guided walks and bike rides, and junior ranger activities. In winter, the park offers easy access to more than 300 miles of groomed and marked snowmobile and cross-country ski trails.

Some of the Indian Creek Unit's 93 campsites ($18–26) have hookups. Two cabins ($50–55) are also available. Other on-site facilities include a camp store, showers, toilets, and an RV dump station. The campgrounds are popular and fill up in summer. Make reservations by contacting the Priest Lake State Park office (314 Indian Creek Park Rd., Coolin, 208/443-2200).

Twelve miles farther north along the east shore, at the mouth of Lion Creek on the lake's northern tip, is the park's **Lionhead Unit** (open summer–fall only). Canadian-born silent-film actor and filmmaker **Nell Shipman** operated a movie studio on this site 1922–1925, producing wildlife and outdoor-adventure films and maintaining a veritable menagerie of 70 animal actors used in the films. Although several of the shorts and features filmed here were successful, the studio's high-overhead operation eventually drove it into bankruptcy. The animals were shipped off to the San Diego Zoo, and Shipman returned to Los Angeles to continue to work in the film industry, though no longer as a star; she died there in 1970. Most of her films have been rediscovered, restored, and assembled in a collection at Boise State University.

Also at the Lionhead Unit is the sunken shell of the *Tyee II* lying in the shallow waters of Mosquito Bay just offshore. The vessel was a steamer tug used to haul large booms of logs from the Diamond Match flume site to the lake's outlet, where the logs were ferried down the Priest River to the sawmill. Towing a full load of logs, the tug managed just 0.5 mph and took some 60 hours to reach the end of the lake. On such a trip, the tug would typically burn 10 cords of wood. The operation lasted until 1959, when the *Tyee* was stripped of its iron and scuttled where you see it today.

The Lionhead Unit campground (47 sites, $16) is smaller than the one at the Indian Creek Unit and less developed; the sites don't have hookups. Hiking trails wind through the woods, across Lion Creek, and out to the beach, where you just might find moose tracks in the sand. The park is also an excellent launching place for boaters heading to Upper Priest Lake.

The **Dickensheet Unit** is the most primitive of the state park's three units, on Priest River south of the lake between Coolin and the road junction with Highway 57. The campground (11 sites, $12) has minimal facilities. It's a great place to kick back with a fishing pole, away from the crowds up on the lake.

OTHER SIGHTS AND RECREATION
Priest Lake Museum and Visitors Center
The informative Priest Lake Museum and Visitors Center (208/443-2676, 10 A.M.–4 P.M. Tues.–Sun. Memorial Day–Labor Day, free), just north of Hill's Resort on Luby Bay, is a good place to begin your exploration of the area. The museum occupies a log cabin built by the Civilian Conservation Corps in 1935. It was originally a residence and office for the Kaniksu National Forest's first ranger. Inside you'll find exhibits on the threatened grizzly bear and woodland caribou—including sand

castings of their tracks—and on rare area plants such as the northern beechfern, deerfern, black snakeroot, and salmonberry.

The most entertaining fact you'll learn here is how the name of the local national forest came to be changed from Priest River National Forest to Kaniksu National Forest. It seems the Forest Service wanted a fresh start after the antics of Priest River National Forest's first supervisor, Benjamin McConnell, gained public attention. McConnell was dismissed for "public drunkenness, habitating with a newly divorced woman, and shooting his pistol in the middle of town." The new name, Kaniksu, was the local Native American term for the Jesuit missionaries in the area. Friendly volunteer docents at the museum are on staff to answer your questions.

Vinther-Nelson Cabin

You'll need a boat to get to this historic log cabin (10 A.M.–3 P.M. Wed.–Sun. summer, free) on Eightmile Island. The cabin was built in 1897 by the Crenshaw brothers, who tried their hand at mining on the island. After a year with no luck, the Crenshaws gave up and sold the cabin to W. J. Anders and family. Anders cleared the land and planted crops but couldn't make a go of it. In 1900 he sold out to two cousins—Sam Vinther and Nels Nelson, who intended to revive the mine and make a fortune; they never struck pay dirt. Nevertheless, the two men and their families continued to live on the island. In 1967 the U.S. Department of Agriculture ordered that all private buildings on Priest Lake's federally owned islands be demolished. The descendants of Vinther and Nelson negotiated an agreement to allow the cabin to remain standing as a historic site open to the public. Inside the cabin you'll find a restored kitchen and a small museum. Outside, trails lead to great views and the old mine site, long since caved in.

Hanna Flats Cedar Grove

This small area just south of the Priest Lake Ranger District office in Nordman (look for signs marking the turnoff to the west) offers a short nature trail in summer, cross-country ski trails in winter, and a soggy, mosquito-infested bog in spring. Pick up the interpretive trail brochure at the ranger station; it explains that one reason these cedars survived is because they weren't considered valuable by early loggers. An interesting subplot dates from the settler days when a man named Gumpp built a cabin here. He moved away for the winter, and when he returned found Jim Hanna and family living in his house. They had come upon the cabin, assumed it was abandoned, and moved in. Gumpp didn't raise a stink; he just moved on.

Beaver Creek Recreation Site

This is the main jumping-off point for hiking, mountain biking, and canoeing to Upper Priest Lake Scenic Area. Once the site of the Beaver Creek Ranger Station, the area offers a campground ($18), a picnic area (day-use $7), a boat launch into the main lake, trailhead parking for the hiker-biker Navigation and Lakeshore Trails, and a 1,600-foot canoe-portage trail directly to the Thorofare. The site is on the lake's northwest shore; turn east on Forest Road 2512 at Nordman and follow it north 12 miles.

Granite Falls and Roosevelt Grove

Actually just over the border in Washington, but reached only via Idaho, the short Granite Falls Trail (Trail 301) leads to views of upper and lower Granite Falls and continues to the Roosevelt Grove of Ancient Cedars. To get to the trailhead, continue north on Highway 57 past Nordman; the road eventually becomes Forest Road 302. Most of the old-growth cedar grove went up in flames in 1926, but about 22 acres are left. The cedars—estimated average age 800 years—are impressive, but it's lower Granite Falls that steals the show. The roaring water rounds a corner at the top of the falls and plummets down a huge granite dihedral. Clever Forest Service engineers have constructed a truly scary viewpoint right out over the cliff edge.

Also at the trailhead is **Stagger Inn Picnic**

Area (free). The area was named by firefighters who used it back in the 1920s as a base camp. At that time, the road up the east shore ended at Nordman, and the firefighters had to hike in from there—a distance of about 14 miles. By the time they got here, they were exhausted, and many had to "stagger in."

On the way back to Priest Lake, don't miss the wacky **Shoe Tree.** You won't believe your eyes. In a gnomish scene right out of a fairy tale, old pairs of shoes completely cover the trunk of a huge cedar just off the highway. The local tradition started decades ago, but no one seems to remember why. If there's a Priest Lake local out there who knows the whole story, please fill me in. The tree is at the short spur to Trails 261 and 264, south of Granite Falls on the west side of the road.

Hiking and Biking

A favorite for hikers and mountain bikers alike is **Navigation Trail** (Trail 291). It begins at Beaver Creek Recreation Site and first enters a dense, fern-filled cedar forest. The trail can be mucky in places, but it's always beautiful. You'll pass an abandoned trapper's cabin before arriving at Plowboy Campground on the southwest shore of Upper Priest Lake. It's an easy three-mile hike to this point. You can picnic and head back from here, or continue north another three miles to Navigation Campground at the upper end of the lake. Between the two campgrounds the trail traverses a wooded lakeside slope, offering great views of the water and mountains at many points along the way. This portion of the trail is also easy. Fit hikers will have no problem hoofing it all the way from Beaver Creek to Navigation Campground and back—a round-trip distance of 12 miles—in half a day.

Beaver Creek is also the trailhead for **Lakeshore Trail** (Trail 294), which heads south along the western edge of the lake for 7.6 miles. It's an easy and popular trail open to both hikers and bikers. Along the way you'll cross five streams, pass numerous campsites, and get great views of the lake.

Probably the most popular and heavily used trail at Priest Lake is the nine-mile **Beach Trail** (Trail 48), which runs right by Hill's Resort, Luby Bay Campground, and several summer cabins. It's open to hikers only—no mountain bikes—and runs between Kalispell Bay boat launch on the north and Outlet Bay on the south. Along the way it meanders through woods and along the beach, jumping back to Lakeshore Road for two short stretches.

Mountain bikers can make best use of the east side of the lake, particularly the northeast shore north of Priest Lake State Park's Lionhead Unit, where numerous gravel roads have been closed to motor vehicles, making ideal mountain-biking country. For starters, try Caribou Creek Road, right out of the Lionhead campground.

For a map of the area and a longer list of trails, stop by the Priest Lake Ranger District office (32203 Hwy. 57, Priest River, 208/443-2512) south of Nordman. You can rent a mountain bike ($25 per hour, $45 half-day, $75 full day) on the west shore at Hill's Resort on Luby Bay (208/443-2551).

Rock Climbing

How can you resist the looming block of **Chimney Rock** on the skyline of the Selkirks above the east shore of the lake? To anyone who has ever strapped on sticky shoes and a harness, this granite monument cries out to be climbed. The 350-foot-high west face is split by several flake and crack systems, offering routes ranging from 5.3 to 5.11b. Access is via Horton Creek Road, which turns east off the lake's east shore road about 2.5 miles south of Priest Lake State Park's Indian Creek Unit. Follow the road all the way to the end and park. It's a one-to two-hour hike up to the base of the rock from there. And as long as you're up there, you might want to check out neighboring **Mount Roothan,** which offers several other good routes. For more information, consult Randall Green's excellent book, *Idaho Rock,* now out of print but available via used book sources.

Floating the Priest River

The 44-mile stretch of the Priest River between Priest Lake and the town of Priest River makes a relatively easy float trip, taken either in segments or one long 14-hour day. The toughest rapids, Binarch and Eight Mile, are rated Class III. You'll also encounter three other Class II rapids along the way. In periods of high water—spring and early summer—the Class III rapids are unsuitable for novices. Later in the summer, the river's average depth decreases to three feet or less, and the slow, lazy stretches dominate; after mid-July, plan on dragging the bottom in places. For more information, contact the U.S. Forest Service Priest Lake Ranger District (32203 Hwy. 57, Priest River, 208/443-2512).

Fishing

Kokanee, cutthroat trout, rainbow trout, mackinaw—Priest Lake is full of scaly dinners-in-waiting. The Idaho Parks and Recreation Department suggests trying the following not-so-secret fishing spots: off East Shore Road about 5–6 miles south of Indian Creek; off the end of Pinto Point; and, for deep trolling, off the Kalispell-Papoose-Bartoe Island group (try a chartreuse crocodile as a trolling lure).

Boating

The west shore resorts all have marinas with boat rentals. In and around Coolin you'll find **Coolin Marine** (2148 Cavanaugh Bay Rd., Coolin, 208/443-2469) and **Blue Diamond Marina** (958 Blue Diamond Rd., Coolin, 208/443-2240) about five miles from town, both of which rent boats.

Free **boat-launching ramps** are available at Coolin and at the Forest Service Luby Bay Campground on the west shore. Ramps that charge a fee can be found on the east shore at Cavanaugh Bay Marina and on the west shore at Priest Lake Marina (Kalispell Bay), Elkins Resort (Reeder Bay), and Grandview Resort (Reeder Bay).

Note: The Thorofare is a no-wake zone, and waterskiing and jet skiing are prohibited in Upper Priest Lake.

Huckleberry Picking

The Priest Lake area is loaded with huckleberries, and the menus of many local restaurants boast huckleberry pies, milk shakes, pancakes, cocktails—you name it. Berry-picking season runs mid-July–October. The berries like the sun, so the best places to find them are in open areas along logging roads and trails, mostly west of the lake. You can pick up a berry-picking map from the U.S. Forest Service's Priest Lake Ranger Station, on Highway 57 just south of Nordman. Remember, bears love huckleberries too. If you hear something big thrashing around in the bushes nearby, it's best to yield dibs on the area.

Cross-Country Skiing

In winter, cross-country skiers and snowmobilers take advantage of the hundreds of miles of groomed and marked trails in the area. About five miles of mostly easy ski trails wind through the Indian Creek Unit of **Priest Lake State Park** on the lake's east shore. Across the lake, **Hanna Flats Cedar Grove** just south of Nordman tracks about four miles of easy loops as well. Heading south toward Priest River, the **Chipmunk Rapids Trail System** offers another 10.5 miles of trails.

ACCOMMODATIONS
Resorts

Several resorts dot the lake's west side. The biggest, plushest, and most popular with the tourist set is the venerable **Hill's Resort** (4777 W. Lakeshore Rd., Priest Lake, 208/443-2551, www.hillsresort.com, year-round, $1,450–3,060 weekly summer) on beautiful Luby Bay. Both *Better Homes and Gardens* and *Family Circle* magazines have named Hill's as one of their favorite family resorts in the country. The Hill family has run the resort since 1946 and offer accommodations in either private cabins or condo-like housekeeping units, most with fireplaces. Amenities include a marina;

© IDAHO DIVISION OF TOURISM

Hill's Resort

swimming areas; tennis and volleyball courts; hiking, biking, cross-country skiing, and snowmobiling trails; a gourmet restaurant; and a lounge with live entertainment in season. In summer, bookings are taken only for stays of a week or longer. Summer rates are in effect from the last Saturday in June until the Tuesday after Labor Day weekend. The rest of the year, rates are about 15 percent lower, and nightly rates are available. Units vary in size, sleeping 2–12 people.

C Elkins on Priest Lake (404 Elkins Rd., Nordman, 208/443-2432, www.elkinsresort. com, year-round) is another full-service resort. Accommodations are in individual log cabins, most with fireplace and all with kitchens, full baths, and separate bedrooms; you need to bring your own soap and towels. The lodge restaurant, overlooking the lake and nicely landscaped grounds, serves top-notch Pacific Rim–inspired cuisine daily in summer and between Christmas and New Year's, with a limited schedule the rest of the year. The Trapper Creek Lounge is one of the west shore's social

hubs, often presenting live music that draws in the locals. Other amenities include a marina, beaches, volleyball, and recreation trails. You must book for a week or longer in peak summer season (early July–late Aug.). Peak season weekly rates range $1,498 for a creek-side cabin that sleeps four to $4,529 for a lakefront cabin that sleeps 14. The rest of the year, rates are about 15 percent lower and a two-night minimum (three nights on holiday weekends) is in effect.

Grandview Resort (3492 Reeder Bay Rd., Priest Lake, 208/443-2433) offers cottages, lodge rooms, and suites with, yes, grand views of Reeder Bay. Amenities include a small swimming pool, a marina with boat rentals, and a bright dining room overlooking the lake. It's open year-round. Peak season rates range from around $90 for a lodge room with one queen bed up to $297 for a private lake-view cottage that sleeps 10. Weekly rates are available, and pets are not allowed.

Inns

The **Inn at Priest Lake** (5310 Dickensheet Rd., Coolin, 208/443-2447, $69–135) is a short distance from the lake and offers little in the way of views. The big hexagonal structure looks something like a stone fort dropped incongruously into the woods. But the inn's modern amenities are welcome and include a year-round heated pool and spa, a restaurant, and a lounge. Spa suites and kitchenettes are available. The inn has a nicely landscaped backyard and is within walking distance of Coolin culture. Pets are allowed for a few extra bucks. The inn's year-round RV park offers 12 nice pull-through sites ($25) with full hookups, including TV. Restroom and shower facilities are available.

In Coolin, the **C Old Northern Inn** (220 Bay View Dr., Coolin, 208/443-2426, www. oldnortherninn.com, $105–165) occupies the former Northern Hotel, a turn-of-the-20th-century haven for travelers to the secluded shores of Priest Lake. The restored two-story wooden structure has antique furnishings and first-class modern amenities. The atmosphere is one of rustic elegance. The beautiful cedar-paneled living room features a stone fireplace and picture windows looking out on the lake. Old photographs and newspaper clippings provide a historical accent. The lake is practically at your doorstep—just a short walk down a wooded slope to the private dock and beach. The four standard guest rooms and two suites all have private baths. Rates include a full breakfast (look for huckleberry pancakes) and afternoon wine and cheese. Children over age 12 are welcome, but pets aren't. Smoking is permitted outdoors only. The inn is on your left just before you come to the Leonard Paul Store and Coolin Marina.

CAMPING

Priest Lake State Park offers 151 campsites at its three units. For information and reservations, contact the state park office (314 Indian Creek Park Rd., Coolin, 208/443-2200).

Forest Service Campgrounds

Forest Service campgrounds ring both lower and upper Priest Lake. Many more are found on two islands out in the lake. All campsites are open mid-May–end of September, weather permitting. Camping is limited to 14 days.

From south to north on the west shore, the campgrounds (about $18) are: **Outlet** (31 sites); **Osprey** (18 sites); **Lower Luby Bay** on the lakefront, and **Upper Luby Bay,** across the road in the woods (54 sites total), with an RV dump station; **Reeder Bay** (24 sites); **Beaver Creek** (41 sites). Reeder Bay, Beaver Creek, and the two Luby Bay campgrounds accept reservations (877/444-6777). For more information, call the Priest Lake Ranger District (208/443-2200).

Four more campgrounds (free) on Upper Priest Lake are accessible only by boat or on foot. On the west side of the upper lake are **Plowboy Campground** (4 sites) at the south end of the lake and **Navigation Campground** (5 sites) on the lake's north end. Along the east shore of the upper lake are **Geisinger's Campground** (2 sites) and **Trapper Creek** (5 sites).

Island Camping

In addition to the mainland campgrounds, the Forest Service maintains extremely popular boat-in campgrounds on Kalispell Island (12 campgrounds and two day-use areas), Bartoo Island (five campgrounds and two day-use areas), and Fourmile Island (one campsite). All are first-come, first-served ($10).

Some of the campgrounds have vault toilets; others don't. Because of the heavy summer use, the Forest Service now requires campers staying at campgrounds without vault toilets to carry and use their own portable toilets while on the island. When they return to the Kalispell boat launch—the most commonly used public boat launch for trips to the islands—a free SCAT (Sanitizing Containers with Alternative Technologies) machine there will clean their portable toilets. The machine works like a giant coin-operated dishwasher, flushing the waste into the mainland sewage system and sterilizing the container.

Island campers are permitted to stay 14 days maximum. Pick up a map to island campgrounds at the Priest Lake Ranger District office (32203 Hwy. 57, Priest River, 208/443-2512).

A Safety Reminder

This is bear country, so keep a clean camp. Dispose of all trash properly and promptly, and don't leave food out on picnic tables.

FOOD

The resort restaurants are safe bets for good grub around Priest Lake. On the west shore, **Hill's Resort** and **Elkins Resort** both have excellent reputations for fine cuisine.

In downtown Priest Lake, locals flock to **Millie's Restaurant and Lounge** (28441 Hwy. 57, Priest Lake, 208/443-2365, lunch and dinner daily) for wood-fired pizzas, hot wings, fish tacos, burgers, and cold beer.

For good comfort food, go to **Ardy's Café** (205 Cavanaugh Bay Rd., Coolin, 208/443-4086, breakfast, lunch, and dinner daily), on the east side of the lake in Coolin. In late summer, this classic diner makes good use of local huckleberries, putting the plump little buggers in pies, pancakes, milk shakes, and more.

INFORMATION

For more information, contact the **Priest Lake Chamber of Commerce** (208/443-3191, www.

priestlake.org). For national forest recreation information, contact the U.S. Forest Service's **Priest Lake Ranger District** (32203 Hwy. 57, Priest River, 208/443-2512). The ranger station is just south of Nordman on the east side of the highway.

North to Canada

NAPLES

From Sandpoint, U.S. 95 continues north toward the Canadian border. Ten miles south of Bonners Ferry is the tiny farming and logging community of Naples. Other than an occasional rowdy night of darts at the Northwoods Tavern, the tiny hamlet is usually quiet as can be. Its setting is magnificent. Just west of town, forested ridges climb in ever-higher waves up into the lofty Selkirk Mountains. The rugged peak of Roman Nose—usually snowcapped well into summer—dominates the skyline, sending several creeks rushing down toward Naples from the alpine snowfields. Heading north from town on the scenic old road, you'll cross one beautiful creek after another. One of these, Ruby Creek, flows past Ruby Ridge just outside town.

Spend some time pulled up to the bar at the Northwoods and you'll quickly get a neatly distilled view of what draws a certain independent breed to northern Idaho. At the very heart of it, there just aren't many other people here. The state's visitors guide dutifully lists population figures for almost every town in Idaho, but not Naples. One suspects the local residents probably like that. And since the economy lives and dies by the logging industry, just about every residence prominently displays a green sign reading "This Family Supported by Timber Dollars." Depending on your point of view, logging might be a topic of conversation to avoid down at the Northwoods Tavern, but there's a lesson to be learned. Even if you're diametrically opposed to the loggers' environmental stance, you can't make the disagreement personal; the people you meet at the

Northwoods—and places like it in little logging towns across the state—are by and large some of the finest, most honest and upfront people you'll ever meet.

Entertainment

Right downtown is the **Northwoods Tavern** (Old U.S. 95, Naples, 208/267-1094, until late daily), the area's social hub. Inside you'll find a couple of pool tables, dartboards, a jukebox, good conversation, and plenty of standard domestic beer.

Camping and RVing

Just north of town on U.S. 95 is **Blue Lake RV Resort** (242 Blue Lake Rd., Naples, 208/946-3361, www.bluelakervresort.com), a large and clean full-facility park surrounding a nice fishing pond. Sites with hookups ($31–45), camping cabins ($49), pole tents ($45), and tent sites ($10) are available. Amenities include a shower facility and a clubhouse with a full kitchen.

BONNERS FERRY AND VICINITY

In 1834, 24-year-old New Yorker Edwin Bonner came west, intent on using his already considerable experience in the retail trade to establish himself as a successful frontier businessman. After opening a department store in Walla Walla, Washington, he passed through Idaho's northernmost reaches and noted that the well-traveled ford of the Kootenai River—used by miners stampeding north to British Columbia's goldfields—needed a ferry. By 1864 he had built his ferry and begun to operate it successfully. Eventually Bonner left the area and settled in Missoula, Montana, where he became a wealthy and powerful merchant and political leader. Despite his departure, the town that grew up here stuck with its original name.

Boundary County Historical Museum

A repository of regional history, the small Boundary County Historical Museum (7229 Main St., Bonners Ferry, 208/267-7720, 10 A.M.–4 P.M. Tues.–Sat. summer, donation), across from City Hall, holds a wealth of historical photos and artifacts. Check out the proud portraits of the Bonners Ferry High School class of 1925—all 20 graduating seniors.

Kootenai National Wildlife Refuge

Before the building of dikes and Montana's Libby Dam tamed the Kootenai River, annual spring floods washed over the valley floor, creating prime wetlands for migratory waterfowl. The dikes made for flood-free farming but took away the wildlife habitat. The 2,774-acre Kootenai National Wildlife Refuge (Riverside Rd., 5 miles west of Bonners Ferry, 208/267-3888, sunrise–sunset daily, office 8 A.M.–4:30 P.M. Mon.–Fri.) was created to mitigate that loss. The refuge is kept flooded with water diverted from the Kootenai River and two local creeks. Today, tens of thousands of waterfowl pass through the refuge every year. A 4.5-mile loop road circles the refuge, and several hiking trails (one is wheelchair accessible) lead to good photo vantage points.

In spring, look for mallards, northern pintails, American wigeon, and tundra swans on their way north. In late summer and early fall, the refuge attracts large numbers of Canada geese. Birdwatchers might also catch sight of bald eagles and ospreys. Among other wildlife occasionally seen: black bears, white-tailed deer, moose, and elk. In all, 230 bird species and 45 mammal species have been observed here.

Lookout

Up in the Selkirks about four miles south of the Canadian border is the rentable U.S. Forest Service **Shorty Peak** lookout (July 1–Sept. 30, $25). It's a 2.5-mile hike to the 15- by 15-foot cabin, perched at an elevation of 6,515 feet. The tower sleeps two and offers panoramic views of Creston Valley and the surrounding peaks. This lookout is in grizzly country, so take all appropriate precautions. For reservations, directions, and more information, contact the **Bonners Ferry Ranger District** (6286 Main St., Bonners Ferry, 208/267-5561, reservations 877/444-6777 or www.recreation.gov).

Rafting

Northeast of Bonners Ferry, the **Moyie River** provides Panhandle rafters with a one-day white-water stretch during its high-water season (Apr.–June). Lots of rock gardens among the Class II–III rapids can make it an interesting ride. **ROW Adventures** (Coeur d'Alene, 208/765-0841 or 800/451-6034, www.rowadventures.com) runs guided Moyie day trips ($90–115) that begin and end in Moyie Springs.

The lazy **Kootenai River** isn't in a hurry to do much of anything. It eases out of Montana into Idaho, wanders aimlessly back and forth up the Purcell Trench, and then crosses the border into British Columbia to feed Kootenay Lake. The Class I float is perfect for leisurely canoeing and wildlife watching, particularly west of town where the river flows past Kootenai National Wildlife Refuge.

Golf

Mirror Lake Golf Course (U.S. 95, 208/267-5314, about $16 for 9 holes) is just south of Bonners Ferry. The popular nine-hole course offers broad, unimpeded views of the Purcell Trench looking out toward Kootenai National Wildlife Refuge. Cart and club rentals are available, and ask about local "Stay and Play" packages.

Cross-Country Skiing

The northernmost of the state's Park N' Ski areas, **Snow Creek Park N' Ski** lies 14 miles west of Bonners Ferry. Turn west off U.S. 95 south of town just before the golf course. The turnoff is marked with a sign for the Park N' Ski area. Follow the road west for a short distance, and watch for Snow Creek Road 402 on the right. Snow Creek Road heads north up the valley a couple of miles before branching west once again and beginning its climb into the Selkirks. You'll probably need chains to make it to the trailhead; the road is steep and very icy in places. Parking at the trailhead may consist of no more than one small plowed slot, depending on the good graces of the plow driver.

The well-marked trail system provides a variety of interesting routes. On the Hemlock trail, you'll see numerous examples of the trail's namesake, the delicate mountain hemlock. It was John Muir's favorite tree, easily recognizable by its graceful drooping crown. Another trail, the Toboggan Run, should be avoided by all but expert skiers—it's a long, steep climb on a narrow trail through many trees. If you have climbing skins with you, use them. Otherwise, prepare for herringbone hell. The only thing worse than going up Toboggan Run would be going *down* Toboggan Run. Unless you have a death wish, don't try to descend this trail unless plenty of soft, fresh snow is on the ground to cushion your inevitable face-plant.

Although these trails are high in the mountains, they're not high enough to offer any panoramic views. The trail system here is not extensive: The longest loop will take you just over an hour, about the time it takes to drive to the trailhead from Bonners Ferry in all but the best conditions. Grooming is minimal, and on weekends, snowmobilers will be buzzing about the vicinity.

Accommodations

On the south approach to town is **Bear Creek Lodge** (5952 Main St., Bonners Ferry, 208/267-7268, $60–110), which offers 12 guest rooms, a hot tub, a full-service restaurant, and complimentary continental breakfast.

On the north end of town, two miles north of the Kootenai River on the west side of U.S. 95, is the **☾ Bonners Ferry Log Inn** (43 Tobe Way, Bonners Ferry, 208/267-3986,

www.bonnersferryloginn.com, $50–94). Even though the inn is right along the highway, it's farther away from the hustle and bustle than the motels on the south side of town. The beautifully landscaped grounds, warm, comfortable guest rooms, and toasty hot tub will combine to drop your blood pressure off the bottom end of the sphygmomanometer.

The largest and swankiest lodging in town is the **Best Western Kootenai River Inn and Casino** (7169 Plaza St., Bonners Ferry, 208/267-8511 or 800/346-5668, from $139 d). The inn is owned by the local Kootenai tribe, and for better or worse, Indian gaming is here to stay. Slot machines and bingo in north Idaho may seem tacky, but the money the gambling operation sucks in helps keep the tribe alive. In any case, the inn boasts the best location in town and offers all the finest amenities. Some rooms under $100 are available. The inn's restaurant overlooks the river and offers upscale fare and outstanding ambience.

Paradise Valley Inn (621 Treetop Bluff Lane, Bonners Ferry, 208/267-4180 or 888/447-4180, www.paradisevalleyinn.com, year-round, from $89) offers elegant and comfortable B&B accommodations on a secluded 64-acre spread 10 minutes southeast of town. Views from the modern ranch house are impressive, and all five guest rooms have private baths. Rates include a big breakfast served inside or out on the log porch. To reach the inn, take Paradise Valley Road east off U.S. 95 at the stoplight in Bonners Ferry and follow the signs for 3.5 miles.

Food

A rare treat awaits discriminating diners in Bonners Ferry. **☾ Alberto's** (6536 S. Main St., Bonners Ferry, 208/267-3410, 8 A.M.–9 P.M. daily, entrées $10–16) is a superb gourmet-caliber Mexican restaurant, among the very best in Idaho. Alberto hails from Mexico City, bringing with him his favorite recipes from central Mexico. Everything on the small but artful menu is made from scratch. Try the heavenly Azteca, a baked concoction consisting of layered corn tortillas, shredded chicken, cheese, and an out-of-this-world homemade mole. Carne asada and camarones (shrimp), separately or together, are other specialties of the house. Entrées come with excellent tortilla chips, salsa, and soup. Choose from six Mexican *cervezas,* all served in chilled mugs.

At the Kootenai River Inn, **The Springs Restaurant** (7169 Plaza St., Bonners Ferry, 208/267-8511, breakfast, lunch, and dinner daily, dinner entrées $12–20) offers upscale atmosphere, an eclectic menu of steaks, seafood, poultry, and pastas, and great views of the Kootenai River.

When the need for caffeine calls, **The Creamery Café** (6426 Kootenai St., Bonners Ferry, 208/267-2690, 8 A.M.–4 P.M. Mon.–Fri.) answers with a gamut of espresso drinks. In addition to great high-octane joe, you can also get sandwiches, frozen yogurt, and other goodies. The smell of fresh-made waffle cones beckons halfway down the block.

Information

The **Bonners Ferry Chamber of Commerce Visitors Center** (U.S. 95, 208/267-5922, www.bonnersferrychamber.com) is in the parking lot across the highway from the Kootenai River Inn. It's usually closed in winter, although if you drive by, you might find someone there. The U.S. Forest Service **Bonners Ferry Ranger District** office (6286 Main St., 208/267-5561) is on the south edge of town. They can hook you up with recreation information.

U.S. 95 TO EASTPORT

U.S. 95 leaves Bonners Ferry heading north, following the Kootenai River for a time. Then it branches east, winding its way through the Purcell Mountains to the Canadian border crossing at Eastport. For much of the way you drive through a veritable tunnel of trees. Several nice lakes line the route, but they're all sheltered from view.

Camping

At **Smith Lake,** anglers will find a boat ramp and a small lake full of rainbow trout, bass,

BORDER CROSSING REGULATIONS

As of 2009, U.S. citizens must have a passport or similar document to enter Canada and to reenter the United States after their visit. The U.S. Department of Homeland Security's Western Hemisphere Travel Initiative requires all American citizens returning from Canada, Mexico, and the Caribbean to present one of the following documents: a valid passport, a passport card, an enhanced driver's license, or a Trusted Traveler Program Card (NEXUS, SENTRI, or FAST). To apply for these documents, contact the U.S. Department of State (877/487-2778, www.travel.state.gov). Canadian citizens now need a passport or similar documentation to enter the United States. Citizens of all other countries need passports and appropriate visas to enter Canada and the United States.

Customs regulations for both countries are extensive. Generally, you can transport a limited dollar amount of foreign-bought goods across the border duty-free. Above that limit, you must declare your purchases and pay duty on them.

Some items may require a permit to transport them between the two countries. Red flags immediately rise with firearms and other weapons, pets, agricultural products, and drugs – prescription or otherwise. For customs regulations and information pertaining to the Idaho border crossings, contact the U.S. Customs office in Eastport (208/267-3966, www.cbp.gov), or the Canadian Customs offices at the Idaho border: Kings Gate (250/424-5391) for Eastport and Rykerts (250/428-2575) for Porthill.

and catfish as well as the Forest Service's **Smith Lake Campground** (7 sites, free). To get here, take Smith Lake Road (Forest Rd. 36) off U.S. 95, seven miles north of Bonners Ferry. Another 12 miles down U.S. 95 is Brush Lake

Road (Forest Rd. 1004), which leads to **Brush Lake** and a campground (4 sites, free).

Nineteen miles from Bonners Ferry is Robinson Lake Campground Road (Forest Rd. 449), which leads into large **Robinson Lake** and a campground (10 sites, $8). A two-mile interpretive trail points out the intricate interactions within the forest ecosystem. Boaters note: The boat-launching ramp at Robinson Lake is on the lake's north side, accessed a little farther down the highway. No gasoline motors are permitted on Robinson Lake.

Copper Falls

Take time to stretch your legs at this exquisite spot just a short distance off the highway. Turn east at the Copper Creek campground sign and head down Forest Road 2517 a couple of miles past the campground (16 sites, $6). Be careful of logging trucks. A pullout on the right and a sign on the left mark the trailhead. The easy trail climbs briefly, then traverses a beautiful slope of mixed conifers before descending slightly to the falls. An interpretive brochure, hopefully available at the trailhead, explains the biological points of interest along the way. The falls make a beautiful 80-foot cascade, perfectly proportioned to allow you an up-close look without getting soaked. After crossing the creek, the trail loops back to the trailhead a little lower down Copper Creek—a total distance of less than a mile. Benches are well placed at particularly tranquil spots. Bring a picnic lunch and enjoy an alfresco repast in the cool clean air by the rushing waters.

Eastport

The Eastport border station marks the international boundary between the United States and Canada. It's open 24 hours. Those interested in cultural differences will note that canary-yellow Union Pacific locomotives rub elbows with their cherry-red Canadian Pacific cousins, while the Yankee-sharp U.S. Customs and Immigration building contrasts nicely with its older, more civilized Canuck counterpart. The Moyie River knows no border, however. It flows past unimpeded on the way to its confluence with the Kootenai, some 20 miles to the south as the Canada goose flies.

HIGHWAY 1 TO PORTHILL

From its junction with U.S. 95, Highway 1 continues up the Purcell Trench, past fertile farmland and the Kootenai River on the west and the abruptly steep Purcell Range on the east. The Purcells continue on into British Columbia, Canada. They don't have to stop at the border—but you do. The Porthill border crossing is open 7 A.M.–11 P.M. daily. At Porthill, you might notice the tall trellises of the Elk Mountain Farms hops plantation on the valley floor to the west. The plantation cultivates about 2,000 acres of aromatic hops for use in Anheuser-Busch beers.

www.moon.com

DESTINATIONS | ACTIVITIES | BLOGS | MAPS | BOOKS

MOON.COM is ready to help plan your next trip! Filled with fresh trip ideas and strategies, author interviews, informative travel blogs, a detailed map library, and descriptions of all the Moon guidebooks, Moon.com is all you need to get out and explore the world—or even places in your own backyard. While at Moon.com, sign up for our monthly e-newsletter for updates on new releases, travel tips, and expert advice from our on-the-go Moon authors. As always, when you travel with Moon, expect an experience that is uncommon and truly unique.

MOON IS ON FACEBOOK—BECOME A FAN!
JOIN THE MOON PHOTO GROUP ON FLICKR

MAP SYMBOLS

▦ Expressway	◖	Highlight	✗	Airfield	⚓	Golf Course
Primary Road	○	City/Town	✗	Airport	🅿	Parking Area
Secondary Road	◉	State Capital	▲	Mountain	▲	Archaeological Site
Unpaved Road	⊛	National Capital	+	Unique Natural Feature	⌖	Church
------- Trail	★	Point of Interest				
⋯⋯ Ferry	•	Accommodation	⬙	Waterfall	⌂	Gas Station
Railroad	▾	Restaurant/Bar	⬙	Park	◌	Glacier
Pedestrian Walkway	■	Other Location	⬙	Trailhead	▨	Mangrove
Stairs	Λ	Campground	⛷	Skiing Area	▨	Reef
					▨	Swamp

CONVERSION TABLES

°C = (°F - 32) / 1.8
°F = (°C x 1.8) + 32
1 inch = 2.54 centimeters (cm)
1 foot = 0.304 meters (m)
1 yard = 0.914 meters
1 mile = 1.6093 kilometers (km)
1 km = 0.6214 miles
1 fathom = 1.8288 m
1 chain = 20.1168 m
1 furlong = 201.168 m
1 acre = 0.4047 hectares
1 sq km = 100 hectares
1 sq mile = 2.59 square km
1 ounce = 28.35 grams
1 pound = 0.4536 kilograms
1 short ton = 0.90718 metric ton
1 short ton = 2,000 pounds
1 long ton = 1.016 metric tons
1 long ton = 2,240 pounds
1 metric ton = 1,000 kilograms
1 quart = 0.94635 liters
1 US gallon = 3.7854 liters
1 Imperial gallon = 4.5459 liters
1 nautical mile = 1.852 km

MOON SPOTLIGHT COEUR D'ALENE & THE IDAHO PANHANDLE

Avalon Travel
a member of the Perseus Books Group
1700 Fourth Street
Berkeley, CA 94710, USA
www.moon.com

Editor and Series Manager: Kathryn Ettinger
Copy Editor: Christopher Church
Graphics Coordinator: Kathryn Osgood
Production Coordinator: Lucie Ericksen
Cover Designer: Kathryn Osgood
Map Editor: Albert Angulo
Cartographers: Kat Bennett, Kaitlin Jaffe, Chris Henrick, and Andrea Butkovic
Previous Edition Updater for Moon Idaho: Julie Fanselow

ISBN: 978-1-59880-830-8

Front cover photo: Coeur d'Alene Lake © Jfergusonphotos | Dreamstime.com

Title page photo: © Idaho Division of Tourism

Printed in the United States

ABOUT THE AUTHOR

James P. Kelly

Boise resident James P. Kelly has loved big mountains ever since his childhood in Seattle. As a restless teenager, he spent countless hours in the North Cascades exploring alpine lakes and trails beaten out by miners' boots.

Before moving to Idaho in 2000, James had only traveled through the Gem State en route to Montana, Wyoming, Colorado, and the Dakotas. He eventually returned to live in this land of rugged mountains, mystical deserts, and vodka-clear trout streams. To help seal the deal, he even married a third-generation Idahoan, Dana, whom he proposed to while hiking in the Trinity Mountains.

James, a former chef, earned a communication/journalism degree at Boise State University before becoming the restaurant critic at the *Idaho Statesman*. He has written numerous food and travel-related features for *Northwest Palate* and other magazines and websites.

When he's not hanging out in his vegetable garden with his wife and two kids, Nolan and Audra, James can be found snowshoeing to backcountry yurts, foraging for morels, catching big trout, and dining in Sun Valley restaurants. Check out his travel blog at gemstatejunket.blogspot.com.